Protecting a Woman's Right to Choose

GREAT SUPREME COURT DECISIONS

Brown v. Board of Education
Dred Scott v. Sandford
Engel v. Vitale
Marbury v. Madison
Miranda v. Arizona
Plessy v. Ferguson
Regents of the University of California v. Bakke
Roe v. Wade

ROE
v.
WADE

Protecting a Woman's Right to Choose

Susan Tyler Hitchcock

CHELSEA HOUSE
PUBLISHERS

An imprint of Infobase Publishing

Roe v. Wade

Chelsea House
An imprint of Infobase Publishing
132 West 31st Street
New York, NY 10001

Library of Congress Cataloging-in-Publication Data
Hitchcock, Susan Tyler.
Roe v. Wade : protecting a woman's right to choose / Susan Tyler Hitchcock.
p. cm. — (Great Supreme Court decisions)
Includes bibliographical references and index.
ISBN 0-7910-9239-9 (hardcover)
1. Roe, Jane, 1947—Trials, litigation, etc.—Juvenile literature. 2. Wade, Henry—Trials, litigation, etc.—Juvenile literature. 3. Trials (Abortion)—Washington (D.C.)—Juvenile literature. 4. Abortion—Law and legislation—United States—Juvenile literature. 5. Roe, Jane, 1947—Trials, litigation, etc. 6. Wade, Henry—Trials, litigation, etc. 7. Trials (Abortion)—Washington (D.C.) 8. Abortion—Law and legislation—United States. [1. Trials (Abortion) 2. Abortion—Law and legislation.] I. Title. II. Title: Roe versus Wade. III. Series.
KF228.R59H58 2006
342.7308'4—dc22   2006015136

Series design by Erika K. Arroyo
Cover design by Takeshi Takahashi

Printed in the United States of America

Bang EJB 10 9 8 7 6 5 4 3 2 1

This book is printed on acid-free paper.

·EQUAL·JUSTICE·UNDER·LAW·

Contents

Meet Jane Roe

Norma McCorvey knew the telltale signs. She woke up with a vague sense of nausea, which gnawed at her insides all day long. Her breasts felt swollen and tender to the touch. She couldn't make it through the day without naps, and it was hard to get up in the morning. In part, it was depression; nothing had gone right for her all her life. Norma McCorvey knew it was something else, too, however. She was pregnant—again.

Norma was 21 years old, and this was the third time she had had these feelings. She couldn't bear to face the future. She had nowhere to turn. "There was this thing growing inside of me, getting bigger every day, and I couldn't push the terrible fact of it out of my mind," she wrote in her autobiography more than

20 years later. "I didn't want to give birth to another unwanted child."[1]

McCorvey had experienced a painful childhood, with an abusive mother and a father who rarely came home. She had no contact with the two children she had already borne. The first was five years old, living with Norma's mother, who had essentially kidnapped the child before she was a year old. The second would now be walking and talking, but Norma had never even held that baby; she gave it up for adoption at birth.

Now, another baby was growing inside her. Norma McCorvey had no family support, no steady income, no stable home—nothing that she thought a child deserved. She was, she wrote later, "a deadbeat bum, a twenty-one-year-old nobody."[2] She must have looked back on her life and saw how many wrong turns she had taken to get where she was in that winter of 1970.

A ROUGH CHILDHOOD

Norma McCorvey grew up in a little Louisiana town 60 miles north of Baton Rouge. Built along the Atchafalaya River, Lettesworth had as many shacks as wood-frame houses, as many outhouses as flush toilets. Not even the main street was paved. Norma's mother had Cajun and Cherokee blood, and Norma's fondest childhood memories were of her mother's grandmother, who "smoked a corncob pipe, made her own soap, and boiled her washing in a big iron kettle in the front yard."[3] Norma's father, Olin Nelson, learned radio electronics during World War II and ran his own radio and television repair service. Rumors were that his mother had been married 13 times and had once run a house of prostitution. She certainly acted the part: Norma remembered how her paternal grandmother dyed her hair flame red, drove a sleek Lincoln Continental, and made money as a fortune-teller.

Norma's older brother, Jimmy, was mildly mentally disabled. "He wasn't very good at learning things," she recalled, "so

I had to walk him to school and teach him how to ride a bike and throw a ball and play baseball."[4] No matter how hard Norma tried, though, she always got in trouble with her mother:

> She called me stupid, and an idiot, and when she was angry, which was just about every time she saw me, she smacked me so hard my head hurt. I never could figure out why she disliked me so. Sometimes I felt she blamed me for Jimmy being slow. Or simply for being a girl. . . . Sometimes she would lock me up in a closet in the dark for hours, so I could figure out what I had done wrong. My answers were never the right ones. Then she would get so mad that sometimes she would leave the house and not return to let me out for hours.[5]

Olin Nelson didn't seem to notice how his wife treated their daughter. He kept telling Norma he would take her fishing, but he never did. The family moved to Dallas, Texas, but Norma's home life only got worse. Her father spent more and more time in his TV repair shop, and her mother spent more and more time in the bars.

At the age of 10, Norma stole money from a gas station where she worked and convinced a friend to hop a bus to Oklahoma City. They lied their way into a hotel room and lived there for almost two days, ordering hamburgers and fries from room service. Eventually, the hotel manager discovered them. When the police came, Norma's friend accused her of kissing and touching her all over. Norma did not deny it, but she said her friend had asked her to. Soon her future was in the hands of a judge.

"Norma, I've got half a mind to send you to the State School for Girls," McCorvey remembers the judge saying. He sent her to a Catholic boarding school instead, to become "a moral and honest citizen."[6] But Norma broke all the rules and ended up at the State School for Girls, after all. She lived there from age 11 to 15, later remembering those as the happiest years of her childhood. Her teachers disciplined her, but they also encouraged her. "You've got brains," one teacher told her. "If you concentrate on one thing you can really get ahead."[7] Sent home, Norma got into trouble each summer, so back she went to reform school year after year. After three years, her favorite teacher warned her that she would go to jail instead.

DREAMS AND NIGHTMARES

Tragically for Norma McCorvey, what happened next was even worse than jail. Her mother contacted a relative, a man who ran a locksmith shop, who agreed that Norma could live with him. From the first night on, he raped her. "I tried to fight him off, but he was much too powerful," wrote Norma years later. "After a few days I stopped fighting. And then I was ashamed of myself for giving in. Much too ashamed to tell anybody or ask anybody for help."[8]

Every night, she used her willpower to blank out what he was doing, but every morning, she woke up crying and cursing. She felt trapped, hurt, and helpless. Finally, her mother visited and could tell that something was wrong. She asked about the dark circles under Norma's eyes, and Norma told her the truth. Norma's mother confronted the man, who laughed and ordered them both out of his house. Long after, Norma wrote, "Although this man sometimes appears in my nightmares, I never saw him again."[9]

Norma found herself out of the frying pan but into the fire: She moved back home with her mother and her mother's boyfriend. She got a job at a drive-in hamburger stand where waitresses roller-skated out to the cars to take orders. Most of the girls she worked with were in love or engaged. When they talked about their sexual experiences, Norma couldn't join in. She was on the one hand numbed by her memories of forced sex and on the other hand ignorant about romance. Then one day, into the drive-in charged a souped-up, shiny old black Ford Fairlane, and Norma met the man who would help her catch up with her friends in romance, sex, and marriage. His name was Ellwood Blanchfield McCorvey III. People called him Woody.

After a few dates, Woody told Norma he wanted to sleep with her. She thought he just wanted to lie down side by side. She remembers that Woody "smiled, took me inside, and showed me exactly what he meant."[10] Soon Norma began doubting what they were doing. "I don't want to do this anymore," she told Woody. "I want to be married."[11] He finally agreed, and on June 17, 1964, they were married in Dallas. He wore jeans, a white shirt knotted at the waist, and flip-flops. She wore a black blouse and stretch pants. Because she was only 16, she needed her mother's signature to get married. "It was one of the worst mistakes I've ever made," Norma McCorvey later wrote. "I did it with no more thought than I'd give now to a new sofa or a set of tires."[12] Norma McCorvey got very little romance out of the deal.

After they married, Woody wanted to move to California. He was a sheet-metal worker and thought he could get more work there than in Texas. They drove to his parents' home in Pasadena, and his mother wouldn't let Norma in the door without seeing their marriage license. At that point, Woody became lazy. He didn't look for work; he just drove his mother around doing errands. Evenings erupted into yelling. Then Woody came up with a plan. Norma sang well, so they would sell the Ford Fairlane, move to Hollywood, and Norma would become a star.

The vision faded as soon as they got off the bus. Woody got a job, and they rented a tiny apartment. Then Norma started feeling queasy in the morning. Her breasts felt sore, but she didn't know why. "Oh my God, honey," Norma remembers her neighbor, Ruth, saying. "You're pregnant."[13]

"That's not so," Woody yelled when he heard. "We're having too much fun."[14] Then he shouted at her, "How could you?" None of his other girlfriends had ever gotten pregnant. He accused her of going with another guy. He kept slapping her and hitting her until finally Norma locked herself in the bathroom. Woody broke in and with one punch knocked her out. Norma McCorvey woke up in a hospital. Ruth helped get her on an airplane to Dallas. Norma had always been frightened of flying, but it was nothing compared to what she had been through.

The last time Norma McCorvey saw Woody, he showed up in her hospital room the day after their daughter was born. Norma screamed. A nurse rushed in, made Woody McCorvey leave, and helped Norma, a 16-year-old mother, feed newborn Melissa. Once they went home to Norma's mother, new tensions developed. Norma resented how her mother took over caring for Melissa, but the only freedom she got was when her mother was watching the baby. Then things went from bad to worse, especially when her mother realized that Norma was socializing only with women. Her favorite nightspot was a lesbian bar, where gay women came to party, seeking friends or maybe sexual partners.

Norma's mother considered her an unfit parent. At the end of a long weekend with friends, Norma came home to find her baby gone. "She was telling me that I'd abandoned Melissa," McCorvey recalled. "She would step in and raise her grand-daughter by herself. . . . Melissa was hers."[15] Norma felt the rage rising. She started screaming at her mother. The police arrived and threatened to arrest her if she didn't quiet down. It felt as if there were no other options. Norma called a friend and moved away—from her mother and her daughter.

FROM BAD TO WORSE

Life didn't get better for years. A friend found her a job in a hospital, working nights. She was falling in love with women, but she said yes to a fellow hospital worker, a man, and got pregnant again. He was willing to marry, but she wasn't. With a rule against out-of-wedlock pregnancy, the hospital fired Norma. Her baby was born but never even shown to her.

After that, she just couldn't pull herself up beyond mere survival. She worked as a manager at go-go nightclubs. She

The *Roe v. Wade* case was much bigger than Norma McCorvey. Pro-choice demonstrators march in Washington, D.C., on November 20, 1971, to demand the legalization of abortion. The *Roe v. Wade* case would be argued in the Supreme Court the following month.

moved into a hippie house. She took and sold drugs, especially amphetamines. She became good at pool and, playing doubles with a man, enjoyed a short winning streak in the Dallas bars until his wife objected. She joined a carnival, where she took care of the animals, and then discovered she was pregnant again. Here she was, a "pregnant redneck hippie carnie from Texas," as she put it.[16] She felt that she couldn't have sunk much lower.

Then a friend told her that there was a medical way to end a pregnancy, but it was illegal. You couldn't just walk into a doctor's office in Dallas and ask him to do it. You had to know someone who was willing to do it secretly. Norma McCorvey asked the doctor who had delivered her two babies about the procedure. From him, she learned the word *abortion*. He didn't do them, he told her, and would report anyone who did.

Someone gave her the address of a clinic where abortions were performed. She found the building, but there was no one inside. "What I saw first was an old, old wooden doctor's examining table sitting abandoned in the middle of a big room," she recalled years later. "The table was dirty. Filthy. So was the whole office. There was dried blood on the floor. And on the examining table. . . . The place smelled horrible." Back out on the street, a passerby told her that the clinic "got busted last week." Then she noticed the police tape, labeling the building a "crime scene."[17]

Someone else gave her the name of a lawyer: Henry Mc-Cluskey. She liked his gentle manner, but he suggested adoption, too. She shook her head. Norma McCorvey was absolutely determined to get an abortion, whether he would help her or not. That made McCluskey distressed, Norma McCorvey wrote. "He looked me straight in the eye. He told me that illegal abortions were dangerous, very dangerous, and that lots of women got killed when they had them."

To that, Norma answered, "I don't care."[18]

Then Henry McCluskey told Norma McCorvey something that would ultimately shape the course of American law. He knew two young women lawyers who were planning to challenge the Texas law against abortions. They needed a plaintiff, a pregnant woman. Henry McCluskey thought Norma McCorvey might be the person they were looking for.

"Will it help me get an abortion?" she asked him.

Henry McCluskey answered honestly, "I don't know."[19]

EQUAL·JUSTICE·UNDER·LAW·

2

Abortions Past

For as long as anyone can look back in time, women have found ways to end their pregnancies. Ancient books identify herbs and give recipes for teas and salves to bring back the menses (start a woman's menstrual period again). To the ancients, reinstating a menstrual period was another way of saying *abortion*.

Not only have women historically tried to end their pregnancies, but for almost as long as humans have been inducing abortion, there have been rules and laws about it. Abortion has always been a topic of debate and concern. Is it right or wrong for a woman to end the life of a fetus growing inside her? Is it right or wrong to help a woman abort? At the same time that ancient herbalists and physicians were recording their knowledge, ancient lawmakers were recording opinions on the subject. All took the subject seriously, but not until the last two centuries were laws written down that forbade abortions altogether.

ANCIENT OPINIONS ON ABORTION

Documents from long ago show the use of *abortifacients,* a word that means "substances taken to induce an abortion," from the Latin words *abortio,* "untimely birth" or "miscarriage," and *facio,* "I make" or "I do." A famous passage in the book of Exodus, dating back earlier than 1000 b.c., suggests the ancient Hebrew view of abortion:

> When people who are fighting injure a pregnant woman so that there is a miscarriage, and yet no further harm follows, the one responsible shall be fined what the woman's husband demands, paying as much as the judges determine. If any harm follows, then you shall give life for life, eye for eye, tooth for tooth, hand for hand, foot for foot, burn for burn, wound for wound, stripe for stripe.[20]

This passage describes the case wherein two men are presumably in some sort of fistfight and one of them hits a nearby pregnant woman in such a way that she has a miscarriage. If she comes through safely, the crime is between her husband and the man who hit her, to be repaired by an exchange of money. If she is hurt or killed in the process, however, the penalty matches the damage and could even mean death.

The scene differs so much from what we would call abortion today that it is hard to apply its principles. Many see this passage from the Bible as the earliest statement of abortion law, however. In our day, lawyers would say that the two possible outcomes represent the difference between civil and criminal law. If a miscarriage is the only result, the husband's personal property—his unborn child—has been damaged. The act is a

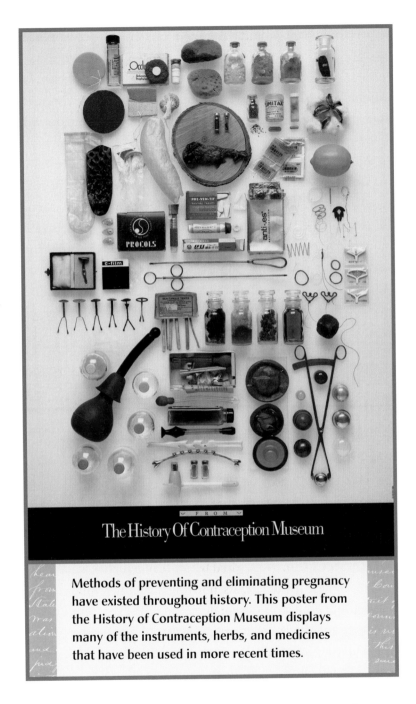

▽ F R O M ▽

The History Of Contraception Museum

Methods of preventing and eliminating pregnancy have existed throughout history. This poster from the History of Contraception Museum displays many of the instruments, herbs, and medicines that have been used in more recent times.

crime against him as a person, and he has a right to be paid money to compensate for his loss. That rule fits today's definition of a civil suit. If the woman is hurt or killed in the process, the act is considered criminal, not civil—a crime against society, not just against the other man. In that case, according to Hebrew law, the attacker deserved to be punished in body. In modern times, criminal punishment involves imprisonment or, in extreme cases, execution. In modern times, though, the state and not the victim exacts the punishment.

Applied to abortion specifically, the passage from the book of Exodus crystallizes the central problem of the law and ethics of abortion: Which being is more important, the woman or the growing life inside her? To the ancient Hebrews, the safety and survival of the woman had the greater value, because the consequences of causing a miscarriage were lighter than the consequences of hurting or killing the woman. Not all cultures, philosophers, or judges have agreed on this central question, however.

Literature from the ancient world, written hundreds of years before the birth of Christ, sometimes discusses abortion. In Plato's *Republic*, the ancient Greek philosopher explained how he believed humans could make society the best it could possibly be. For him, individuals held value only as far as they contributed to making society better. He considered abortion useful in achieving the best society. He believed that a society should follow certain rules about who could have children and when, but "if they are unable to prevent a birth," they can "dispose of it on the understanding that we cannot rear such an offspring."[21] For Plato, society as a whole held a higher value than the single unborn child, and sacrificing the fetus could be justified if it contributed to the greater good of the community.

Other ancient philosophers presented different ideas. Doctors to this day follow the Hippocratic Oath, rules of ethics to be followed by medical practitioners. The oath follows the philosophy of an ancient Greek doctor named Hippocrates, born in the fourth century b.c. No one knows a lot about where Hippocrates lived or even who he was, but he inspired generations of ancient Greek physicians to see medicine as a rational science and not as superstition or even as religion. The Hippocratic Oath states basic promises that every doctor ought to make: I will honor my teachers, I will share my knowledge, I will keep the sick from further harm, and I will keep my work confidential. Few doctors today have trouble following any of these four rules. The last part of the Hippocratic Oath is more controversial in our time, though. It says, according to a famous translation made in the 1940s, "I will neither give a deadly drug to anybody who asked for it, nor will I make a suggestion to this effect. Similarly I will not give to a woman an abortive remedy. In purity and holiness I will guard my life and my art."[22] For this ancient Greek, so different from Plato, those entrusted with the practice of medicine should hold life itself as sacred. Nothing they do should contribute to death, either at life's beginning or at life's end.

Since the 1940s, doctors and philosophers have asked whether this translation faithfully translates the Hippocratic Oath. Beyond that, many question whether modern physicians can, or should, follow the rules expressed in this part of the oath. Doctors still agree to the Hippocratic Oath as they graduate from medical school, but most contemporary versions do not mention abortion at all.[23] Nevertheless, the traditional Hippocratic Oath remains an important landmark in the history of beliefs about abortion. It expresses a fundamental belief in the value of the life of the growing fetus that has guided medicine and influenced law for centuries.

Plato and Hippocrates represent the two extremes in the age-old debate over abortion. Another ancient philosopher found a middle ground in the discussion. Philo, an Egyptian philosopher who lived at the time of Christ, had read both the Hebrew and the Greek texts. He believed that it was important to consider how far along in the nine-month period of her pregnancy a woman was when discussing abortion. Philo distinguished between a fetus "still unfashioned and unformed" and a fetus that "had assumed a distinct shape in all its parts." The more mature fetus, Philo wrote, should be considered a fully formed human

Hippocrates medic?

Hippocrates is considered the father of medicine. His writings and practices were the first to bring a scientific approach to medicine.

being, even though it is "still in the workshop of nature, [but] like a statue lying in a sculptor's workshop, requiring nothing more than to be released and sent out into the world."[24]

Philo did not have today's scientific understanding of how an embryo develops. He looked back to the ancient philosophers to define the moment when the fetus could be considered a living being on its own. The Greek philosopher Aristotle had written that in the early stages a growing embryo had a "vegetative soul." Later, the fetus developed a "rational soul." Philo used these ideas and became the first to express the idea that human life begins at some time between the fertilization of the egg and the birth of the child. Early Christian thinkers, including the influential thirteenth-century theologian St. Thomas Aquinas, adopted this concept. They believed that the fetus became "ensouled" at a midpoint in its growth inside the mother's body. Such an idea influenced beliefs and laws about abortion for centuries. The challenge was to determine when that turning point occurred.

ABORTION IN ENGLISH LEGAL HISTORY

Historically, U.S. law developed out of English common law—certain old laws of England dating from before a.d. 1000, before such things were written down. It is called the English common law because it evolved from the rules followed by everyday people, or commoners. Beginning in the eleventh century, those rules were recorded in writing as law. Even in those days, people were struggling to write down rules by which to determine when the fetus inside the womb gained the status of human being.

A law recorded in the late twelfth century reads as follows:

> First the man's brain is formed in his mother's womb, then the brain's surface with a layer is covered in the sixth week.... In the second month the veins are formed.... In the third month he is a man without a soul. In the fourth month he is in limb steadfast. In the fifth month he is quick & grows, & his mother is witless, & then the ribs are formed, then befalls her manifold sorrow as the burthen is bumping up against her womb.[25]

Within this colorful language lies the beginning of the English rule for determining when a fetus becomes a human being. At the beginning of the fifth month of gestation, the mother is "witless," or without knowledge of the baby growing inside, for she still cannot feel any movement within the womb. A month later, though, she can feel the fetus—her "burthen," or burden—because she feels the movement of legs and arms "bumping up against her womb" from inside. With the "quickening," or beginning of movement of the unborn child, comes the mother's "manifold sorrow," which will continue until she gives birth.

"Quickening," or the point at which the movements of a fetus can be felt inside the mother's womb, became an important idea. Once a fetus had quickened, it was a human being to be protected under the law. "If there is anyone who strikes a pregnant woman or gives her a poison which produces an abortion, if the foetus be already formed or animated, and especially if it be animated, he commits homicide," reads one book of law from the thirteenth century.[26] "A woman also commits homicide if, by a potion or the like, she destroy the ensouled child in her womb," reads another written soon after.[27] Yet another labeled abortion "a great misprision, but no murder."[28] Although the word *misprision* could simply mean "mistake," in legal terminology, it means "misdemeanor"—in other words, a crime deserving lighter punishment as compared to a crime such as homicide, which the law calls a felony and that requires a stiff sentence.

In early English law, in other words, abortion was a kind of murder if it happened after the so-called quickening of the fetus. Modern medicine has, of course, developed more sophisticated ways of describing embryonic development, but doctors still pay close attention to the time when the pregnant woman first notices a growing fetus's movements. It normally happens between the sixteenth and eighteenth weeks of gestation. If you divide the nine months of pregnancy into three equal periods, called trimesters, the biological process of quickening normally occurs early in the second trimester. Since English common law, this turning point in a pregnancy has been an important idea in discussions of abortion, yet no consistent use of the idea predominates. Early written opinions so contradict themselves, in fact, that when Justice Harry Blackmun wrote the 1973 Supreme Court decision in the case of *Roe v. Wade,* he found it "doubtful that abortion was ever firmly established as a common law crime, even with respect to the destruction of a quick [or quickened] fetus."[29]

The first modern statute, or rule enacted by the government, against abortion came in 1803. It was a time of government crackdowns in Great Britain. British noblemen had watched the French Revolution with horror. They feared that their countrymen might also rise up and overthrow the men in

WHAT IS AN ABORTION?

Abortion occurs when an embryo or fetus growing inside a pregnant woman leaves the uterus, severing its biological ties with the mother's body and ending its development. Many abortions happen naturally. Deliberate abortion—the intentional manipulation of the embryo or fetus with a goal of ending the pregnancy—can be accomplished chemically or mechanically.

The most common chemical abortive in use today is Mifeprex, also known as RU-486 and nicknamed the morning-after pill. Mifeprex blocks the action of progesterone, the female hormone most active during pregnancy. It changes the chemical nature of the lining of the uterus so that it no longer adequately provides the embryo with nourishment and oxygen. Three days after a woman takes Mifeprex, she may take another drug, misoprostol, which causes uterine contractions and expels the contents of the uterus. This chemical abortive procedure must be used within the first seven weeks of pregnancy.

During the first trimester, or first three months, of pregnancy, three surgical methods of abortion are currently in use. If pregnancy is detected early, a woman can undergo a menstrual extraction, which involves suctioning out the contents of her uterus, including the lining and the implanted embryo. Later, a more complex suction and aspiration procedure may be performed. An alternative later procedure is called dilation and curettage (D&C), in which the physician dilates the cervix, making room to introduce a loop-shaped knife into the uterus and scrape out its contents.

power. Members of Parliament enacted a number of new laws to place tighter controls on those they thought might threaten the status quo. The 1803 statute—called Lord Ellenborough's Act, after Edward Law, Baron of Ellenborough and Britain's lord chief justice at the time—clustered a number of crimes and labeled them felonies. They included malicious shooting, shooting, stabbing, cutting, wounding, and setting buildings on fire. The act also named as a felony "the malicious using of Means to procure the Miscarriage of Women."[30] Anyone who "shall wilfully, maliciously, and unlawfully administer to, or cause to be administered to . . . any deadly Poison, or other noxious and destructive Substance or Thing, with Intent . . . to cause and procure the Miscarriage of any Woman then being quick with Child" would be considered to have committed a felony. Even in cases when so-called quickening could not be proven, abortionists would be considered felons. They would receive lighter punishment, such as fines, imprisonment, exile—or, in a punishment that combined personal shame and physical torture, they could be "set in and upon the Pillory," a wooden frame that locked them, head and hands, in place, and "publickly or privately whipped."[31]

Although legal experts struggled to write rules defining the starting point of human life, medieval herbalists were dispensing herbal remedies to help women control their reproductive cycles. Folklore identified herbs that could cause the menstrual flow—in other words, end a pregnancy and return a woman's monthly periods—or that could expel a fetus, alive or dead. Many a pregnant woman asked another woman, versed in herbal lore, for help in ending an unwanted pregnancy, instead of going to an educated male physician. The tradition of going outside the male medical establishment for abortions stretches far back into time. As the established systems of law and medicine gained power and influence in society, herbal methods of abortion came under attack. Some herbal abortionists were accused of being witches who worked in concert with the devil and against the laws of God and nature.

   The early Christian church adopted Philo's view that early in pregnancy a fetus could not yet be considered a human being. In the twelfth century, Pope Innocent III, one of the most influential popes of the Middle Ages, decreed that after quickening, abortion equaled the sin of homicide. That rule was echoed by Pope Gregory XIV in 1591, who ordered excommunication from the Catholic Church for anyone performing an abortion after quickening. In 1869, Pope Pius XI went even further. In a decree that renounced any type of birth control, he commanded that the church abandon the distinction between what he called the "ensouled" and the "unensouled" fetus in its consideration of abortion. The intentional death of a fetus at any stage, from the moment of conception on, was the same as infanticide (killing an infant). In the United States, the principles of the Roman Catholic Church or any other religious group do not hold sway in a court of law. Church and state stay separate by U.S. law, and the job of a judge is to know and uphold the laws of the nation. In the United States, as elsewhere around the world, however, church definitions and religious guidelines influence behavior and opinion. Debates in the public forum over abortion have always raised questions of religion as well as law.

ABORTION IN AMERICA

In the Puritan American colonies, any behavior that strayed from childbirth within marriage was considered a sin. Unwed mothers faced fines, whipping, or public shaming; those who aided them in abortion faced equally severe punishments. Abortions took place but remained secretive. The first abortion brought to legal trial in U.S. history occurred in Massachusetts in 1812. U.S. law still used the rule of quickening to judge the legality of an abortion, and the court dismissed the case, for no accuser could prove that the fetus had quickened.[32] Individual states began to pass laws against abortion: Connecticut in 1821, Missouri in 1825, Illinois in 1827, and New York in 1828. These laws targeted the abortionist, not the woman. The laws were not drawn up in the spirit of a moral judgment against the woman seeking abortion, but instead were designed to protect her from reckless, untrained practitioners. In 1828, New York State revised its law to allow for a "therapeutic exception," making abortion legal when it "shall be necessary to preserve the life of such woman, or shall have been advised by two physicians to be necessary for such purpose."[33]

By the middle of the nineteenth century, abortion was a common topic of heated debate. On the one hand, as medical professionals learned more about reproduction and fetal development, they claimed pregnancy and childbirth as their area of expertise. One Pennsylvania doctor, Hugh Hodge, wrote a paper on obstetrics that was distributed widely. He called abortion a crime. It is the professional obligation of the physician, wrote Hodge, to "regard the infant, as well as the mother, from

Elizabeth Cady Stanton and her daughter, Harriet. from a daguerreotype 1856.

Elizabeth Cady Stanton was an American feminist who did not advocate abortion. Instead, she believed that granting full rights and liberties—such as voting—to women was the way to elevate their station in society.

the period of conception to delivery." He compared the fetus to a chick growing inside the egg: "not only a living, but an independent being" with "a spiritual existence."[34] Doctors across the country became concerned about the number of abortions causing physical harm and even death. When a young, unmarried woman was found dead in a Boston boardinghouse in 1845, the victim of an infection contracted during an abortion, doctors felt even more urgently that they should protect women from unprofessional practitioners. The American Medical Association, founded in 1847, soon gained a strong voice in the debate over abortion.

On the other side, American women in the late 1800s were uniting to fight for their own concerns. Early feminists like Elizabeth Cady Stanton advocated a woman's right to "voluntary motherhood," recognizing that the burden of raising a large family often limited a woman's access to the freedoms promised by American society. Female abortionists, none of them trained physicians, offered services secretly for hundreds, probably thousands, of women. Ann Trow Lohman called herself Madame Restell, "professor of midwifery." She sold contraceptives and performed abortions on women in New York City for almost 40 years. She was arrested many times and spent a year in prison. Her work came to an abrupt end thanks to Anthony Comstock, founder of the New York Society for the Suppression of Vice, which was dedicated to purging the city of what its members considered immoral behavior. Comstock trapped Lohman into selling him contraceptives and then had her arrested under a federal law that forbade the sale of obscene literature or other articles for immoral use. Her case never went to court, however, because on the morning of the trial, Ann Trow Lohman killed herself.

The debate was heating up, and the stakes were getting higher. By the first decades of the twentieth century, every state in the Union had passed a law against abortion. At the same time, women were organizing to press for rights on many different fronts. They wanted to be able to vote; they wanted equal educational opportunities, including graduate and professional degrees; they wanted better pay and better working conditions; and they wanted to control their own reproductive destinies.

3

The Challenge

A lot happened in American history between the 1920s and the 1960s, but as far as abortion law was concerned, not much changed. Men dominated the practices of law and medicine, and with few exceptions, both professions stood firmly against the practice of abortion. Women from the 1920s on had waged campaigns in an effort to make contraceptives, as well as access to abortions, more available to women. Margaret Sanger, for example, a Catholic woman from upstate New York, began working as a nurse around 1910 in the poor neighborhoods on the Lower East Side of Manhattan. Sanger soon became convinced that working-class women needed to be able to control the number of children they bore.

An early pioneer of reproductive rights, Margaret Sanger fought to make birth control available to women and founded what is now Planned Parenthood.

As an illustration, Sanger often told the story of a woman she had helped named Sadie Sachs. No doctor would provide Sachs with contraceptives. Her husband, a truck driver, would not use condoms. With three children already, and having a hard time feeding and clothing them, Sachs was horrified to find herself pregnant again. After attempting her own abortion, she almost died from infection. Sanger began caring for her, carrying food and water up three flights of stairs, and nursed her back to health. Not longer after that, Sadie Sachs, finding herself pregnant again, attempted another abortion. This time she died—in Margaret Sanger's arms.

Fueled with passion to save the lives of women like Sadie Sachs, in 1916 Margaret Sanger opened the first birth control clinic in the United States. She wrote books and articles, traveled the country lecturing, founded the world's first scientific journal on birth control, and fought to change public opinion about women's reproductive rights. Her efforts reached around the world. She helped organize a World Population Conference in 1926, drawing attention to the links between overpopulation and reproductive planning. Women deserve "to choose the time and conditions best suited for fulfillment of the maternal function," she argued in her 1928 book, *Motherhood in Bondage*.[35] Sanger inspired the 1942 founding of the Planned Parenthood Federation of America, an organization that continues to this day to promote family planning through contraception and abortion.

Doctors began to reconsider their position on birth control and abortion. A book came out in 1936, written by a doctor and read by many others, reporting that 680,000 abortions had occurred in 1935 in the United States. Almost all of them, wrote the author, were responses to "economic distress."[36] A handful of doctors dared to practice outside the law. Many without professional degrees, often women, offered abortions secretly. One woman, Ruth Barnett, had apprenticed with doctors but did not have a medical degree herself. She ran an abortion clinic for more than 30 years in Portland, Oregon. Doctors whispered her name and address to pregnant women who came into their offices. Law officials and police officers knew about her business, but they left her alone. She was, as one historian puts it, "clean, efficient, and safe—a valued member of an underground and criminal profession allowed to flourish."[37] Between 1929 and 1953, Barnett provided abortions for hundreds of thousands of women.

Margaret Sanger opened the first family planning clinic in the United States, pictured above, in Brownsville, Brooklyn. The clinic was raided, and Sanger was arrested.

In short, the reality of abortion practice did not match the laws on the books. Something had to give. The first sign in American courts that abortion law might change occurred in Massachusetts in the 1940s. When Daniel R. Wheeler and his wife learned that she was pregnant, they soon agreed that it would be best for her to terminate the pregnancy. She had been mentally unstable for years. Pregnancy, childbirth, and the years of childcare that would follow might unbalance her psychologically, sending her to extremes of mental illness that neither of them wanted to consider. Wheeler was a physician, so he had the knowledge, equipment, and drugs needed to perform an abortion. He inserted an abortifacient

into his wife's womb with a rubber tube and effectively in-
duced an abortion. The procedure caused undue bleeding,
and ultimately, Mrs. Wheeler needed hospital care. Hospital
officials brought the abortion to the attention of state officials. A judge found Wheeler not guilty. The state appealed.
The Massachusetts Supreme Court affirmed the lower court's
decision, saying: "An abortion is not unlawful if performed to
save life or health, including mental health, and if performed
upon the best judgment of the doctor performing it, if his
judgment corresponds with that of the average of the doctors
in the community."[38]

Over the next 15 years, cases similar to this one came up in
a number of other states, and the spirit of the law about abortion shifted subtly. When a woman's pregnancy occurred as the
result of rape or incest, judges tended to be more lenient. When
the woman's life would be threatened by going to full term
with the pregnancy or giving birth, judges tended not to deem
abortion a crime. When the woman's health would be threatened—and here, the definitions varied from physical health to
mental health, as in the case of the Wheelers—judges granted
leniency. Scares about fetal deformity swept the country in the
late 1950s and early 1960s as it became known that thalidomide,
a drug commonly prescribed for morning sickness during pregnancy, could cause traumatic birth defects, severely stunting or
deforming the trunk, limbs, and digits of the child for life. The
community of doctors, mentioned in the *Commonwealth v.
Daniel R. Wheeler* decision, carried a voice in the matter. Major
city hospitals appointed committees to interview each woman
as she requested an abortion—a development that actually re-
duced the number of abortions performed in hospital settings.
Meanwhile, a multitude of abortions continued off the record
and outside the law. No one knows how many abortions were
performed during the 1950s and 1960s. Estimates range from
the hundreds of thousands to more than one million American
women per year.

A new ethic of abortion was emerging, but each state had its own set of conditions and guidelines. The American Law Institute, a nonprofit dedicated to clarifying the law, proposed that all state laws follow basic guidelines that allowed abortion if the mental or physical health of the mother was at stake, if the pregnancy was a result of rape or incest, or if fetal deformities had been detected. To question these limits, individuals had to bring lawsuits against the officials acting in support of these laws. Many such cases surfaced during the 1960s, with two in particular paving the way toward the suit of Jane Roe against the state laws of Texas. Those two cases occurred in Connecticut and California.

GRISWOLD V. CONNECTICUT, 1965

Access to birth control was an issue that moved parallel to, but often out in front of, the changing laws about access to abortion. Although the Roman Catholic Church stood solidly against any form of birth control drugs or devices, in 1961 the National Council of Churches of Christ, a nationwide partnership of Protestant churches, not only declared its official approval of birth control methods but even called it a "positive duty" that married couples assess their ability to support a family and plan childbirth accordingly.[39] Only the state of Connecticut still had a law, dating back to 1869, banning the use of, sale of, and distribution of information on contraceptives. For that reason, through the early 1960s, Connecticut was a hotbed of protest against restrictive laws about the reproductive rights of men and women. In the 1940s and again in the late 1950s, doctors practicing in New Haven—both were professors at Yale University, as well—brought suit against the state, describing situations in which their medical judgment would have led them to recommend contraceptives for a patient while their state law prohibited them from doing so.

Both cases resulted in the doctors' suits being dismissed. One went to the U.S. Supreme Court, resulting in the case of *Poe v. Ullman,* argued before the court in March 1961 and

The 1925 Sixth International Neo-Malthusian and Birth Control Conference, organized by Sanger (third from right) and held at the Hotel McAlpin in New York, brought together leaders in eugenics and birth control.

decided on June 19, 1961. Justice Felix Frankfurter wrote the decision, stating that the case did not present "a collision of actively asserted and differing claims" in which anyone, either the doctor or his patients, was truly damaged by restriction of their constitutional rights. "The true controversy in this case is over the opening of the birth-control clinics on a large scale," wrote Justice William Brennan, concurring with the decision. "It is that which the State has prevented in the past, not the use of contraceptives by isolated and individual married couples. It will be time enough to decide the constitutional questions urged upon us when, if ever, that real controversy flares up again."[40]

Justice Potter Stewart did not agree with the decision, and he wrote a dissenting opinion that emphasized the rights of a couple to make reproductive decisions privately. "The State is asserting the right to enforce its moral judgment by intruding upon the most intimate details of the marital relation with the full power of the criminal law," he stated. "In sum, the statute allows the State to enquire into, prove and punish married people for the private use of their marital intimacy."[41]

Stewart's dissenting opinion, and even Brennan's comment as he upheld the decision, seemed to invite further court tests of Connecticut's laws against birth control clinics. Estelle Griswold, executive director of the Planned Parenthood League of Connecticut, decided to press the issue. In consultation with the same Yale doctor who brought the second suit and failed, C. Lee Buxton, she opened a birth control clinic in New Haven. It was clearly announced as a counseling center for married couples wishing advice on family planning and contraception. Opening the clinic was a conscious and public act of civil disobedience. Griswold and Buxton knew that they were breaking the law, but it was a law they hoped to see overturned. A detective visited the clinic. He was shown around and given information. No one tried to hide the clinic's purpose. Nine days after the clinic opened, state officials arrested Griswold and Buxton. They were convicted in January 1962 and fined $100 each. Their case was appealed up to Connecticut's Supreme Court, and the judgment against them upheld. They continued to press on, and the U.S. Supreme Court agreed to hear the case in March 1965. The record documenting the Supreme Court decision begins as follows:

> Appellants, the Executive Director of the Planned Parenthood League of Connecticut, and its medical director, a licensed physician, were convicted as accessories for giving married persons information and medical advice on how to prevent conception and, following examination, prescribing a contraceptive device or material for the wife's use. A Connecticut statute makes it a crime for any person to use any drug or article to prevent conception. Appellants

THE CONCEPT OF A LEGAL PRECEDENT

Underlying the judicial system of the United States is a strong faith in the Constitution as a universal and ageless document and a supremely wise foundation for all future decisions. Every amendment—continuation or clarification officially added to the Constitution—links back to the original language and fundamental ideas. It is the job of every judge and every lawyer to know the Constitution thoroughly. When a lawyer represents a client, saying that she or he has suffered a wrong, it is that lawyer's responsibility to refer to the Constitution and its amendments and to identify exactly what injustice has been committed. When a judge pronounces a decision, the explanation must come directly from language written in the Constitution.

Such has been the case now for more than 200 years in U.S. history. Many a court decision has been spoken, written, and recorded, referring to the original Constitution and offering an updated interpretation of the ideas expressed in it. Harmonious with faith in the Constitution is faith in the past decisions of judges, particularly those of the U.S. Supreme Court, the highest court in the land. A lawyer can build on others' arguments by referring to the language in a court decision of the past.

Those decisions are called legal precedents—the related cases that came before. U.S. law practitioners believe in a theory called *stare decisis,* Latin for "to stay with what has been decided." In other words, today's decisions build on the wisdom of decisions past. To become a lawyer, students learn hundreds of cases from years, even centuries, ago. When it comes time to argue or judge a case, they must identify legal precedents that connect to the issues of the present day.

claimed that the accessory statute as applied violated the Fourteenth Amendment.[42]

In the discussion of the Supreme Court's final decision on the case of Estelle Griswold, Justice William O. Douglas wrote an important statement about how ideas in the U.S. Constitution work. After looking back through a number of related cases decided by the court, he stated that "specific guarantees in the Bill of Rights have penumbras, formed by emanations from those guarantees that help give them life and substance."[43] In other words, when words in constitutional amendments specifically name certain rights, they imply a related penumbra, or halo, of closely related rights that may not be mentioned by name. That implied cluster emanates, or arises, when the specific right is named. While privacy is nowhere specifically named in the Bill of Rights, wrote Justice Douglas, it is implied in several amendments and therefore protected by the U.S. Constitution. "Would we allow the police to search the sacred precincts of marital bedrooms for telltale signs of the use of contraceptives?" he asked rhetorically. "The very idea is repulsive to the notions of privacy surrounding the marriage relationship."[44] The convictions of Estelle Griswold and C. Lee Buxton were overturned, and the Connecticut law against the use or prescription of contraceptives was termed unconstitutional.

CALIFORNIA V. BELOUS, 1969

Leon Belous, a respected Los Angeles physician, had been practicing medicine for more than 30 years. He had made public statements against the California laws on abortion, which dated back to 1850 and considered the procedure legal only when pregnancy or childbirth presented a life-and-death threat to the woman involved. A young woman, whom the record identifies only as Cheryl, saw Belous on television. She heard him speak out in favor of changing the law to allow women to choose abortion. She and her boyfriend had just discovered that she was pregnant. They were not married—they would marry soon after these events—and they were not prepared to raise a baby. They called the television station to get a phone number for Belous, then made an appointment, believing he would help them get an abortion.

At first, Belous testified, he declined her request, following state law. Cheryl and her boyfriend both became highly emotional in his office. Cheryl cried, and her boyfriend shouted out that she would go to Tijuana, Mexico, for an abortion if she couldn't get one in Los Angeles. Belous knew firsthand that Tijuana abortions were dangerous and expensive. He felt it was his obligation to protect his patient's health. Finally, he handed Cheryl a phone number for Karl Lairtus, a Mexican doctor living

William O. Douglas served as a Supreme Court justice for 36 years, the longest term in the history of the court. Besides his work on the *Griswold* case, Douglas is also famous for his involvement in the plight of convicted American spies Julius and Ethel Rosenberg.

in California, whom Belous knew would perform an abortion in a careful, sterile, and safe manner.

State police were already on the trail of Karl Lairtus. They raided his office just after Cheryl's abortion had been performed. Notebooks they found in Lairtus's office led them back to Leon Belous, whom they arrested and charged with two felonies: abortion and conspiracy to commit an abortion. The state of California accused Belous of aiding Cheryl in getting an abortion—which was equivalent in the eyes of the law to performing the abortion himself—and also of receiving a fee from Lairtus for sending Cheryl to him. Belous denied the second charge. He did not deny the first, but argued that he had helped to save Cheryl from the physical dangers of a Tijuana abortion. Court records show that Belous believed that Cheryl and her boyfriend were so upset that they would "do anything to terminate the pregnancy, which might involve butchery in Tijuana or self-mutilation," and that he "believed that if the young couple carried out their threats, Cheryl's very life was in danger."[45] The lower court in California found Belous guilty on both counts in 1967. He was fined $5,000 and put on two-year probation. He paid the fine but appealed probation.

Next, the case was argued before the Supreme Court of the State of California, and it proved to be an interesting one. To explain their decision, the judges of the California Supreme Court began by quoting the law that had been in force in California for more than a century. They had to compare Belous's actions with the language of the law. Section 274 of the California Penal Code state the following:

> Every person who provides, supplies, or administers to any woman, or procures any woman to take any medicine, drug, or substance, or uses or employs any instrument or other means whatever, with intent thereby to procure the miscarriage of such woman, unless the same is necessary to

preserve her life, is punishable by imprisonment in the State prison not less than two nor more than five years.[46]

In essence, the court decided that a key phrase in this passage, "necessary to preserve," was too vague to allow a clear decision as to whether Dr. Belous's actions were legal. Childbirth did involve the risk of death, and so aiding a woman in avoiding childbirth could indeed preserve her life. The California law put doctors in a difficult ethical position. "The pressures on a physician to decide not to perform an absolutely necessary abortion are, under section 274 of the Penal Code, enormous,"[47] they wrote. The doctor can either risk breaking the law or avoid the risk by sending the woman away, knowing she might choose an alternative solution leading to physical harm or death. As in the Warren decision regarding *Griswold*, the California judges suggested a penumbra of rights emerging from those expressed in specific words. "The fundamental right of the woman to choose whether to bear children follows from the Supreme Court's and this court's repeated acknowledgment of a 'right of privacy' or 'liberty' in matters related to marriage, family, and sex," read the ruling. "That such a right is not enumerated in either the United States or California Constitutions is no impediment to the existence of the right."[48] Therefore, the court decreed, the law was unconstitutional, and Dr. Leon Belous was not guilty.

Sometimes, court decisions lag far behind changes going on in society, and such was the case in the state of California. By the time the Supreme Court ruled on the *Belous* case, the state legislature had rewritten the language of the penal code to allow abortions to preserve either the health or the life of the pregnant woman. By the late 1960s, abortion services were available in California hospitals and clinics. Women traveled hundreds, even thousands, of miles to California to obtain a safe, legal abortion. It was one more step in the long process toward the Supreme Court decision in *Roe v. Wade.*

EQUAL·JUSTICE·UNDER·LAW·

4 Making a Federal Case of It

It was not good news when Sarah Ragle discovered she was pregnant at the age of 22. She had ambitions. Her sights were set on a career in law. She wasn't married, although she and her boyfriend, Ron Weddington, had talked about it. He had made it very clear to her, though, that he did not want to have children. In addition, her parents, if they found out, would be disappointed in her. In 1967, young women simply did not have children without being married, and mothers did not continue on career paths once they had babies.

Born and raised in Texas, the daughter of a Methodist minister, Ragle had high moral principles. She had graduated from high school at the age of 16 and from college at the age of 19.

By 1967, she was already in her last year of law school. It hadn't been easy being 1 of only 5 women in a class of 125 law students at the University of Texas, but she was strong-willed and determined to succeed. She knew that it wasn't the time of her life to have a baby.

She knew as well, though, that according to Texas law, a doctor performing an abortion could be sent to jail for up to five years. Some offered abortions, nonetheless. Rumors went around in her high school about the clinic in downtown Vernon, near the Oklahoma border, where a doctor secretly performed abortions in a back room. The topic of abortion was in the papers a lot. California's legislature had recently made abortions legal, but it was still something you whispered about. Considering the thought of having an abortion made Ragle feel scared and ashamed. "Abortion was something I had never talked about with friends or family," she wrote. "Fortunately, Ron was not as humiliated about this as I. He offered to make some calls."[49]

Sarah Ragle was lucky. Her boyfriend was with her all the way. They pooled their money to come up with the $400 that they needed to pay the Mexican doctor Ron found. They drove south, checked into a motel and then crossed the border into the little town of Piedras Negras. "I can still see Ron and me following a man in brown pants and a white guayabera shirt down dirt alleys to a small white building," Ragle remembered later. She liked the doctor who greeted her and relaxed a little. As the anesthetic began to put her under, she remembers having just two thoughts: "I hope I don't die, and I pray that no one ever finds out about this."[50]

A year later, Sarah married Ron Weddington. He soon entered law school, and Sarah started working for one of her favorite professors. The job was a project for the American Bar Association, the national lawyers' organization, helping to write a new Code of Professional Responsibility. They lived in Austin, Texas, one of the university towns across the country where

Sarah Weddington poses with (l-r) her husband, Ron; Texas Congressman George Mahon; and her mother on the day Weddington argued the *Roe v. Wade* case.

women were beginning to gather and talk about their changing roles and opportunities in American society. It was a time of social concern and outcry on three different fronts. Through demonstrations and protest marches, people showed the strength of their beliefs: Black citizens deserve full civil rights, women should be accepted as equal citizens, and the war in Vietnam should be ended. Sarah Weddington found friends among the journalists who published *The Rag,* a radical newspaper that supported student protests and the antiwar cause. It also took up the cause of women. Women's bodies, lives, and futures had too long been controlled by men, argued articles in *The Rag.*

A favorite book of Sarah Weddington and her friends was *Our Bodies, Ourselves,* an anthology of articles about women's health and sexuality put together by the Boston Women's Health Collective. Even though it was printed on newsprint and stapled together, it was like a bible of the women's movement, with chapters on birth control; abortion; appearance and self-image; sexuality; sexually transmitted diseases; and violence against women, including rape. These were topics that no one had talked about—until now, the late 1960s, when women began talking about them together. Weddington and her friends found the book so inspiring that they formed a women's health collective of their own. Officially, they called it the Women's Liberation Birth Control Information Center, but among themselves they called it the "referral project." If doctors weren't going to give information and advice on birth control, sexuality, and abortion, then women would provide it for one another.

Sarah Weddington was the lawyer in the group, and questions about the law on contraceptives and abortion went straight to her. She realized that not one of the courses she had taken during three years of law school had focused on the legal issue of abortion. She began looking for cases that had been argued and decided in her state and others that could relate to laws about abortion. The more she studied, the more vague the Texas law prohibiting abortion seemed to be.

Getting to know the abortion laws in each of the states, Weddington saw them falling into three categories. There were the restrictive laws—like those of Texas—that declared abortion illegal in almost any circumstance. In the case of Texas, for instance, only an abortion "procured or attempted by medical advice for the purpose of saving the life" of the woman involved could go unpunished.[51] Then there were the more liberal laws, which allowed abortion when the woman had become pregnant through rape or incest, when it was medically determined that the fetus was deformed, or when the life or the health of the woman would be threatened by the birth of a baby. Finally, by 1970, there were two states,

California and New York, whose legislatures had declared abortion a legal medical procedure.

Abortion law remained strictly a state-by-state matter in 1970. There were two ways to change the restrictive Texas law, Weddington and her friends understood. They could either work to convince the Texas legislature to revise the state law, which they considered a long shot. Alternately, they could bring the state law to court, arguing that it contradicted the U.S. Constitution and the nation's Bill of Rights. Researching further, Weddington found that cases had recently been argued before the U.S. Supreme Court that could shed light on the abortion question. The more she read, and the more she talked with others about women's rights, the more the women in Austin believed they could make a solid argument against the Texas law on abortion.

BUILDING UP TO THE CASE

Sarah Weddington studied every detail of the two important court decisions that offered precedents in which state abortion laws had been questioned: *Griswold v. Connecticut* in 1965 and *California v. Belous* in 1969. The Connecticut case involved birth control, not abortion, and the California case involved a doctor, not a woman seeking an abortion; but the outcomes of each carried strong implications about an American citizen's right to privacy in matters of sexuality, childbirth, and reproductive planning.

In the *Griswold* decision, Justice Douglas had written,

> We deal with a right of privacy older than the Bill of Rights. The present case, then, concerns a relationship lying within the zone of privacy created by several fundamental constitutional guarantees. And it concerns a law which, in forbidding the use of contraceptives rather than regulating their manufacture or sale, seeks to achieve its goals by means having a maximum destructive impact upon that relationship. Such a law cannot stand.[52]

He also cited a 1928 decision that protected what a famous Supreme Court justice, Louis D. Brandeis, had termed "the right to be let alone."[53] Whereas the Connecticut case suggested that rights of privacy were protected at the federal level, the California case showed that state laws prohibiting abortion could be questioned.

It was happening across the country. Statutes in the District of Columbia, for example, allowed abortion to preserve a woman's life or health. A case brought against physician Milan Vuitch tested the vagueness of that language. Vuitch argued that many of his patients deserved abortions for the sake of their psychological well-being and that mental health deserved to be as important a rationale for performing an abortion as physical health. Lawyers for Vuitch called the D.C. statute unconstitutionally vague, in the same way that the California Supreme Court had found their statute to be in the trial against Belous. Lawyers for the District of Columbia requested that the Supreme Court hear the case.

The groundswell was encouraging. A friend proposed to Sarah Weddington that they consider testing abortion in the Texas courts, too. Momentum started building. All signs pointed to Weddington herself as the lawyer best positioned to research and argue the case. "My mind whirred with all the reasons I was not the right person," Weddington remembered more than 20 years later in her autobiography, *A Question of Choice.* At first, she worried she would lose the case, but then she realized that every challenge, win or lose, contributed to the larger cause. She called a law school friend, Linda Coffee, and suggested that they work together on the case. Coffee had been a clerk for a federal district judge in Dallas; she knew how appeals and federal courts worked. She agreed to join the effort. "We began to talk of a Texas effort as one to add to the momentum of the litigation strategy others had already put in motion," Weddington wrote later. "We never thought we were filing our own Supreme Court case."[54]

Linda Coffee, Sarah Weddington's cocounsel in McCorvey's trial, prepares for a case in 1972. "I would have guessed the question of abortion would be pretty passé now," Coffee has been quoted as saying recently.

ARGUING THE CASE

Sarah Weddington, the woman who ultimately stood before the U.S. Supreme Court as Jane Roe's lawyer, knew her arguments before she knew her client. Once she and her associates in the Austin women's movement had decided to take on Texas abortion laws in court, their first task was to find a plaintiff. You could have a lot of good ideas about what was wrong with a law on the books, but to present those arguments in a courtroom, you needed a real person whose rights were currently being hindered by those restrictive abortion laws. They found one: a married woman from Dallas who was struggling with a health problem and had been advised by her doctor not to get pregnant and not to use birth control pills. She and her husband worried that their alternate method of contraception might fail, and they wanted assurance in the Texas courts that they could seek a legal abortion. At about the same time, Henry McCluskey told Sarah and her friends about Norma McCorvey, the woman he had met who was desperately seeking an abortion. A meeting was arranged between the three women—McCorvey, Weddington, and Coffee. "I found her street-smart and likable," Weddington recalled. "Her hard-luck stories touched a sympathetic chord."[55] Weddington and Coffee proceeded to plan a lawsuit on behalf of the couple and the single pregnant woman. For the sake of anonymity, they renamed their clients Mary and John Doe and Jane Roe. They filed two lawsuits on March 3, 1970. "Our petitions were straightforward and only three legal-size pages in length," Sarah Weddington remembers. She adds,

> We asked the court to do two things: first, to declare or state that the Texas laws against abortion were unconstitutional on their face, that is, as one could see by merely reading them; and second, to enjoin, or stop, the enforcement of those statutes. In essence, we wanted the court to say the Texas anti-abortion laws violated the U.S. Constitution and to tell the local law enforcement officials to quit prosecuting doctors under those statutes.[56]

The legal grounds on which they made these claims had to do with the vague and unconstitutionally broad language used in the Texas abortion laws, which kept women from receiving adequate medical advice, jeopardized their fundamental right to decide whether to bear children, and compromised their rights to life and privacy. Coffee and Weddington specially requested a three-judge court, which was an option when a lawsuit claimed that the state law contradicted federal law. They presented the

Henry Wade is photographed in his office in the 1970s. The Texas lawyer was already known by the public for prosecuting Jack Ruby for the murder of John F. Kennedy's assassin, Lee Harvey Oswald.

lawsuit against Henry Wade, who had been Dallas County's elected district attorney (DA) for 35 years. Considered a strong, effective civic leader, Wade was the Dallas DA when President John F. Kennedy was shot in that city on November 22, 1963. He would have prosecuted Lee Harvey Oswald for murder had not nightclub owner Jack Ruby shot and killed Oswald; he did eventually prosecute Ruby and had him sentenced to life in prison.

Wade was certainly a powerful person in the city and the state. An odd scene was lining up: a figurehead of the establishment, backed up by an office of 130 attorneys and numerous other legal assistants, would soon go head-to-head with two brash, young women lawyers. A trial date was set for May 22, 1970. Weddington and Coffee added to their petition two affidavits—testimony written out, signed, and sworn to be true by someone who did not plan to speak in court in person. One was a statement by Jane Roe, who did not want to appear in court. She was due to give birth at any time. The other was a report from Paul Trickett, director of the student health center at the University of Texas. He noted that his staff counseled on average one pregnant young woman every day and that well over half of them wanted abortions.

In the weeks before the trial, Weddington and Coffee decided to make their suit a class action, which means they would be representing not just Jane Roe and Mary Doe, but all individuals in similar situations—all women in Texas, in other words, who desired legal abortions. They cheered when they heard that Federal District Judge Sarah T. Hughes, the woman for whom Linda Coffee had once worked, would hear the case. Joining Hughes would be Federal District Judge William M. Taylor and Federal Circuit Judge Irving L. Goldberg. The threesome seemed a favorable mix of judges—likely to take them seriously, even to agree with them—thought Linda Coffee and Sarah Weddington as they put final touches on the arguments they planned to present before the court.

The plan was that, to begin, the two lawyers would split the time and the argument as they spoke before the judges' bench. Linda Coffee began. She had 13 minutes. She focused on the constitutional rights that were denied a woman by the laws restricting abortion. She named six different amendments, five of them in the Bill of Rights—the First, Fourth, Fifth, Eighth, Ninth, and Fourteenth Amendments—that were contradicted by laws against abortion. "I don't think it makes any difference . . . whether you say that the rights involved are First Amendment rights or Ninth Amendment rights," Coffee told the judges. "They involve fundamental human freedom."[57]

Federal District Judge Sarah T. Hughes was on the panel that heard arguments in the first *Roe v. Wade* trial. Hughes is famous for swearing in President Lyndon Johnson on Air Force One after the assassination of John F. Kennedy.

Sarah Weddington argued that, in the history of cases decided in courts of the United States, the fetus growing inside a mother's body had never been regarded as a person with constitutional rights. "I would like to draw to the court's attention the fact that life is an ongoing process," she stated. "It is almost impossible to define a point at which life begins or perhaps even at which life ends." She quoted a former Supreme Court justice, Tom Clark, who wrote, "To say that life is present at conception is to give recognition to the potential rather than the actual."[58]

An attorney for the state spoke, questioning whether it was legal for Jane Roe to bring suit against the state. No woman had ever been arrested or charged for having an abortion, he pointed out. She did not stand to suffer under the law. Furthermore, she was probably not even pregnant anymore, since the suit was filed in March, was being heard in late May, and would be decided sometime in the future. The judges had an answer for that argument. They pointed to famous cases of the 1950s involving the rights of black children who had attended segregated schools. When those decisions were made, some of the children had even graduated from college, but it was still important to complete the judicial process. Judge Hughes referred to *California v. Belous,* asking the state's attorney whether Texas law could also be considered too vague to be constitutional. He answered that he believed it was a medical, not a legal, matter. A second attorney for the state addressed the issue raised by Sarah Weddington, asserting that it was the job of the state to protect every citizen, "in whatever stage it may be in," and that "the state's position will be, and is, that the right of the child to life is superior to that of a woman's right to privacy."[59]

THE VERDICT IN TEXAS

Sarah Weddington left the Austin courthouse on May 22, 1970, feeling dejected. "Because the judges had interrupted constantly, I did not feel I had been able to make my points as clearly as I should have," she wrote later. "I hurried and my conclusion was weak. . . . I was too inexperienced to know that a lawyer very seldom leaves a courtroom feeling confident about what the court's decision will be."[60] All she could do, however, was wait.

The court announced its decision nearly a month later, on June 17. They declared Texas law "overbroad," "vague," and therefore unconstitutional. "Freedom to choose in the matter of abortions has been accorded the status of a 'fundamental right,'" the decision stated.[61] The court did not, though, answer the second request expressed in the lawsuit, which was to order the Texas authorities to stop prosecuting doctors for performing abortions. The women seeking abortions were protected, but the doctors were not. Dallas district attorney Henry Wade publicly announced he would keep arresting and bringing to trial any doctors in his jurisdiction who were performing abortions.

From Sarah Weddington's point of view, the battle was only half won. She and Linda Coffee began making plans to appeal, and for once, they had Henry Wade to thank. "It was procedurally possible to go straight to the Supreme Court if a lower federal court had declared a state law unconstitutional yet local authorities continued to enforce the law," wrote Weddington. "It was the one moment we cheered Wade: Thanks to him, that was the exact situation here."[62] They began preparing the documents required to appeal the decision in *Roe v. Wade* at the federal level.

EQUAL·JUSTICE·UNDER·LAW·

5

The Arguments

During the 18 months between June 1970, when the decision was made to appeal *Roe v. Wade* to the U.S. Supreme Court, and December 1971, when the case was presented, the abortion issue was constantly in the news, not only in America but around the world. In New York, the state legislature had broadened state laws. Abortions were freely available in hospitals and clinics. "Abortion Requests Outrun Operations," read a *New York Times* headline late in July.[63] An estimated 69,000 abortions, most costing $100 or less, took place in New York City alone during the first six months of legalization.[64] Women from all over the nation were traveling to New York for safe, legal abortions. The city was soon dubbed the "abortion capital of the country."[65] Planned Parenthood published a booklet, distributed nationally, that advised women on how and where to obtain legal abortions in the United States.

Marches, demonstrations, and public events in support of legalized abortion took place across the country and around the world. In countries such as France, Great Britain, Canada, Russia, and Taiwan, abortion law was an issue on the minds of the public and the lawmakers. More than 300 prominent French women—including world-famous feminist author Simone de Beauvoir, novelist Françoise Sagan, and actresses Jeanne Moreau and Catherine Déneuve—signed a petition in April 1971, stating that they had received illegal abortions and urging the French government to legalize the procedure.[66] Speaking to Catholics around the world, the pope denounced abortion "as a throwback to barbarism and paganism," as one reporter phrased it.[67] Even in Italy, though, the seat of Roman Catholicism, the Socialist Party proposed limited legalized abortions.[68]

The early 1970s was a period of ferment across the world and the country. Abortion issues joined with others in the minds of many of the protesters, who demonstrated for equal rights for women in employment and education, for civil rights and racial equality, and for peace instead of the growing war in Southeast Asia. Across U.S. campuses, students conducted antiwar protests in May 1970, assailing the U.S. move to bomb Cambodia despite troop withdrawals from Vietnam. Four people attending a demonstration at Ohio's Kent State University were shot dead as police tried to control the crowd. The event shocked the nation and galvanized the antiwar movement. Angry protesters practically shut down American colleges and universities.

Presiding over the situation in the United States was President Richard M. Nixon, elected in 1968 and eyeing a second run for the presidency in 1972. A villain in the eyes of antiwar protesters, Nixon was still solidly popular among the larger American citizenry. He participated in the abortion debate in two important ways. First, as president, Nixon held the power to appoint Supreme Court justices when necessary. Two justices, Chief Justice Earl Warren and Justice William O. Douglas, had retired in 1969. To replace them, Nixon appointed Warren E. Burger and Harry A. Blackmun. When Congress approved both appointments, most observers predicted a sharp turn toward more conservative decisions, more in keeping with Nixon's Republican philosophy. The appointments, wrote an attorney in a *New York Times* opinion-editorial essay, "have brought to a

President Richard M. Nixon made no secret of his strong views against abortion.

screeching halt the expansion of rights which the Warren Court had accorded to criminal defendants."[69]

Second, amid ever more public debate, Nixon made a statement on abortion in April 1971. Because states historically legislate abortion, Nixon said, he was ordering military hospitals to discontinue any abortion practices that did not match laws in the states in which they operated. Abortion rights advocates saw this as a setback; a year before, military hospitals nationwide had been given permission to offer abortions, suggesting that at the federal level, abortions were acceptable. Now, the president was reversing that order. He backed up the announcement with a personal statement: "While this matter is being debated in state capitals, and weighed by various courts, the country has a right to know my personal views." Nixon continued:

> From personal and religious beliefs I consider abortion an unacceptable form of population control. Further, unrestricted abortion policies, or abortion on demand, I cannot square with my personal belief in the sanctity of human life—including the life of the yet unborn. For, surely, the unborn have rights also, recognized in law. . . . A good and generous people will not opt, in my view, for this kind of alternative to its social dilemmas. Rather, it will open its hearts and homes to the unwanted children of its own, as it has done for the unwanted millions of other lands.[70]

While Nixon's opinion had no official bearing on state law or the Supreme Court decision in *Roe v. Wade*, it certainly carried authority in the minds and hearts of many Americans.

PREPARING THE ARGUMENT

On May 21, 1971, the Supreme Court released its docket for the fall. Listed there was No. 808 *Roe et al. v. Wade*. Slowly it dawned on Sarah Weddington that the work started more than two years before was building to something of national proportions. "The little case that Linda and I had started as volunteer lawyers in response to questions from women at the referral project might well become the vehicle for protecting reproductive rights and freedom of choice for every American woman," she wrote. "The thought was overwhelming—and humbling."[71] Joining Norma McCorvey as plaintiff, called Jane Roe, was James Hubert Hallford, a Dallas physician who had practiced medicine since 1958. He had been indicted for performing abortions for a number of patients, including rape and incest victims; women suffering from cancer; and women infected during pregnancy with German measles, known to have the potential to cause fetal birth defects. Sarah Weddington and Linda Coffee worked with a team of researchers, including Sarah's husband, Ron Weddington, by then a practicing lawyer. Various individuals and organizations offered financial, intellectual, and moral support, especially Roy Lucas, a New York lawyer and founder of a nonprofit called the James Madison Constitutional Law Institute, located in New York City.

Listed alongside *Roe* was a second challenge to a state's abortion laws that the Supreme Court also agreed to consider that fall: No. 971 *Doe et al. v. Bolton, Attorney General of Georgia, et al.* It was a more complicated case than *Roe v. Wade,* with many more plaintiffs. Although Georgia law treated abortions less restrictively than Texas law, a number of regulations and restrictions had to be respected by women in order to qualify to receive an abortion or by doctors in order to qualify to perform an abortion. The woman had to be a state resident, two other doctors had to approve a written medical explanation for her abortion, and the procedure had to take place in certified hospital after the application was reviewed by a hospital committee. Mary Doe was the name given to a pregnant married woman who had unsuccessfully sought an abortion, but joining her in this same lawsuit were physicians, nurses, ministers, social workers, and representatives of organizations working for abortion rights. As in *Roe,* the state courts had found the law unconstitutional but had not ordered law enforcement officials to stop prosecuting.

Working with their legal assistants, Sarah Weddington and Linda Coffee prepared materials for their case to present to the Supreme Court. A background document of 139 pages collected all the records of what had been filed, said, and written in the Texas judicial system regarding the case. The brief, or central lawsuit document, could run no longer than 150 pages by Supreme Court rule, relatively short considering the many directions in which the discussion on abortion and the law had to go. Those working on the case paid close attention to the judges now presiding, analyzing the history of decisions they had written, trends in their voting records, and opinions they tended to hold. They suspected that the opinions of individual judges as expressed in 1965 on *Griswold v. Connecticut* indicated the way they might respond to the issues presented in *Roe v. Wade*. Three new justices had joined the court since then, however, including Nixon's two appointees, who were reportedly conservative and therefore likely inclined to limit access to abortion.

The legal team had to select the most effective lines of argument as the controlling theme of the document they wrote. They focused on the question of whether the constitution guaranteed any rights to an unborn fetus. The Fourteenth Amendment, they noted, protects due process of law for "all persons born or naturalized in the United States," but does not specify those not yet born. In Texas, neither those women who received abortions in other states nor those who self-induced abortions were considered criminals. Hence, the team argued, the state did not in those instances regard the fetus as a person with separate rights. Researching every legal argument and court judgment in which the question had ever come up, the lawyers preparing the Supreme Court brief pointed out that only after birth did an individual gain property rights or insurance benefits. "The State does not require that a pregnant woman with a history of spontaneous abortion go into seclusion in an attempt to save the pregnancy," read the brief. "No pregnant woman having knowingly engaged in conduct which she reasonably could have foreseen would result in injury to the fetus (such as skiing in late pregnancy) has ever been charged with negligent homicide."[72] In short, they rallied every piece of evidence already in the legal record to show that neither the law of the land nor the law of the state of Texas appeared to treat the fetus still growing in the womb as a human being with constitutional rights separate from the mother's.

To supplement their central brief statement, lawyers could submit *amicus curiae* briefs: literally, briefs from "a friend of the court" who may have some information pertinent to the case being considered. On behalf of *Roe v. Wade,* numerous amicus briefs came in, including one representing "millions of American women" and signed by many respected woman professionals including anthropologist Margaret Mead, actress Bess Myerson, and District of Columbia representative Eleanor Holmes Norton. Planned Parenthood, Zero Population Growth, and the Center for Constitutional Rights supplied amicus briefs, as did a group of religious organizations representing Jews, Christians, and Quakers. The final page count reached 500. Weddington remembers that the stack of documents they submitted to the court stood a foot tall.[73]

The brief filed by the state of Texas focused primarily on the argument that an unborn fetus was a human being deserving protection by the state. One section of the brief was labeled "The Human-ness of the Fetus." Lawyers for the state also submitted a description of the stages of fetal development, illustrated by 12 photographs taken with a newly invented intrauterine camera. The prints enlarged the images many times beyond life-size, to reveal details of the forming body. Like Weddington's, the Texas documents included amicus briefs. More than 200 doctors signed one statement affirming that medical evidence supports their belief that "the unborn person is also a patient." Another amicus brief came from attorneys general from five other states with laws against abortion similar to those of Texas.[74]

The hearing date was set for December 13, 1971. The decision was made that, from among all the lawyers involved, Sarah Weddington should present the argument. It was important that a woman present the argument on behalf of all women seeking the right to choose abortion.

ROE'S DAY IN COURT

Norma McCorvey—the real Jane Roe—was not in the courtroom as Sarah Weddington stood before the justices of the U.S. Supreme Court to speak on her behalf. McCorvey knew that the case had reached the Supreme Court, but its outcome no longer had any bearing on her personal life. She had exited the legal scene long ago, as a matter of fact. Henry McCluskey had tracked her down to get her signature on an affidavit on behalf of the Texas lawsuit. Linda Coffee called her up and asked her to come to her office right after the court announced its decision. When Norma McCorvey heard they had won, she thought it meant she could end her pregnancy. Coffee explained that because the state was appealing, Henry Wade was still prosecuting all doctors performing abortions. "But, Norma, what does it matter?" Coffee asked McCorvey, by now six months pregnant. "An abortion has to be performed in the first 24 weeks of pregnancy, and it's clearly too late for you now."[75]

It was a moment of despair and anger for Norma McCorvey. She was furious. She felt double-crossed or forgotten. Worse than that, she had to face the reality that she would give birth to another baby. By the time her child was born, she had arranged for its adoption through Henry McCluskey. At the time that Sarah Weddington was preparing arguments in the case of *Roe v. Wade*, Norma McCorvey had not spoken to her for over a year. She was living with her father. She had attempted suicide. She did not feel any connection to the figure whose life details were being presented in the highest court in the nation. "Jane Roe, whoever she was, couldn't help Norma McCorvey," she wrote some years later, looking back at that empty time in her life.

"Norma McCorvey was a lonely, depressed woman, who needed to get through the next day and the next. And as each new day began, she didn't have a clue about how to do it again. Each new day brought a different problem."[76] None of those details came into the courtroom with Sarah Weddington. As Norma McCorvey wrote later, "This lawsuit was not really for me. It was about me, and maybe all the women who'd come before me, but it was really for all the women who were coming after me."[77]

Wherever Norma McCorvey was at 9:30 on Monday morning, December 13, 1971, her surroundings could not have looked anything like those in which Sarah Weddington found herself. The U.S. Supreme Court chamber is a large room, 82 by 90 feet in dimension, with a lofty 44-foot ceiling. The space, Weddington wrote later, "inspires reverence; it is very formal, yet it also gives a feeling of intimacy. Twenty-four marble columns line two sides of the room; 13 different types of marble appear throughout the room. Its high, ornate ceiling is painted in a sea of color, with gilt and vivid reds and blues." Judges sit at a raised dais made of polished mahogany. Facing the judges are tables reserved for the attorneys arguing the cases. Behind them range about 300 seats, one section for the press and another section for guests and observers. All in attendance must observe rituals of respect and honor, including standing when the justices enter the courtroom. "Oyez, oyez, oyez," calls out the court marshall. "All persons having business before the Honorable, the Supreme Court of the United States, are admonished to draw near and give their attention, for the Court is now sitting. God save the United States and this Honorable Court."

One hour was slated for discussion of *Roe v. Wade*. Of that, Sarah Weddington had half, although she chose to reserve about 10 minutes' time for rebuttal after the opposing side spoke. She had prepared, edited, and memorized an oral presentation, but she knew that the justices could interrupt her at any time and take the conversation in an entirely different direction. Chief Justice Burger cut in first, asking her to relate her case to that of

Chief Justice Warren Burger served on the U.S. Supreme Court from 1969 to 1986. Appointed by Richard Nixon, Burger was a strict constitutionalist. In the matter of the *Roe v. Wade* opinion, Burger sided with the majority.

Milan Vuitch, the District of Columbia physician whose lawyers had argued that vague language allowed him to interpret the district's laws against abortion broadly. Vuitch's case had been considered by the U.S. justices in April, and with a five-to-four vote, his appeal was not granted. The court declared that the D.C. statute language was not unconstitutionally vague. Weddington pointed out that her case sought constitutional rights for a woman seeking an abortion and then returned to the points she planned on making. She emphasized the life-changing impact pregnancy has on a woman's life. She outlined the ways in which U.S. laws do not regard the unborn as deserving of constitutional rights. One justice asked whether Texas law made distinctions between abortions at different stages of pregnancy.

Weddington stuck to the principle that not until birth was a being granted the rights protected by the Constitution.

Jay Floyd, a lawyer from the Texas state attorney's office, represented Henry Wade and the state of Texas before the bench. Floyd began by arguing that since Jane Roe could not possibly be pregnant any longer, the case did not have standing; but the justices argued against his point, saying that the time it took for a case to move through the judicial system was always going to be longer than the human gestation period. Floyd backed up and presented the argument that an unborn child—a phrase he carefully used—was considered a person in the eyes of the law and in the language and intent of the Constitution. The state, he argued, has a compelling interest in protecting "life from the moment of impregnation" and must therefore look to its responsibility to protect the unborn by enacting laws against abortion. When pressed by Justice Marshall to provide scientific data as to exactly when human life begins, Floyd said he didn't know: "There are unanswerable questions in the field."[78] Everyone in the courtroom, even the justices, chuckled, but the answer did not help the argument being waged on behalf of the state of Texas.[79]

NOT OVER YET

As lawyers prepare for their time before the Supreme Court justices, the tension builds and the excitement is palpable. Then, they leave the courtroom, rarely elated, often dejected, and always preparing for a long wait. Justices read material in preparation for hearing arguments, but then they take months of further research, reading, and consideration before declaring their decision on any given case. Word did not reach Sarah Weddington and her fellow lawyers working on *Roe v. Wade* for six more months. When it did arrive, in June 1972, it was not the news they were hoping to hear. "This case is restored to the calendar for reargument," read the notice. "Mr. Justice Douglas dissents."[80] In other words, all Supreme Court judges

DUE PROCESS AND THE FOURTEENTH AMENDMENT

The Fourteenth Amendment to the U.S. Constitution was written and approved in 1866, just after the end of the U.S. Civil War. Abraham Lincoln had signed the Emancipation Proclamation, freeing slaves in the South. Once the Confederacy lost the war, the Union regained lawmaking power over all the states. Congress passed this amendment to ensure full citizenship rights and equitable legal process due to all men, including the recently freed slaves. It was written in the spirit of protecting citizens from their government, both state and federal. The first and central statement of the amendment says the following:

> All persons born or naturalized in the United States, and subject to the jurisdiction thereof, are citizens of the United States and of the State wherein they reside. No State shall make or enforce any law which shall abridge the privileges or immunities of citizens of the United States; nor shall any State deprive any person of life, liberty, or property, without due process of law; nor deny to any person within its jurisdiction the equal protection of the laws.

Three important promises are made in these sentences. The first sentence defines a citizen as a person who is either born in the United States or naturalized. To become a naturalized citizen, someone born in a different country must meet certain requirements, study for and pass a test on the history and laws of the nation, and make an oath of allegiance to the United States, renouncing citizenship ties to their former home country. The second sentence protects citizens from any law that "abridges" or limits their rights as protected by the U.S. Constitution; guarantees court protection for every citizen's rights; and promises equal legal protection for everyone. The rights expressed in this sentence are often abridged to the phrase *due process.*

except William O. Douglas—the one justice Weddington felt sure would support them from the beginning—agreed that they needed to hear the two lawyers present their arguments one more time before making a final decision.

This time, Linda Coffee and Sarah Weddington prepared a 17-page brief. They filed a few amicus curiae briefs to go with it. In the document, they were able to report that in the first nine months of the year 1971, 1,658 Texas women had gone to New York and received abortions. They dug more deeply into the difficult question of when a developing human gains constitutional rights. "'When life begins' is an individual leap of faith that no one can prove," Weddington finally decided. "We could find no substantial legal peg for maintaining that rights began prior to birth. Although we were not entirely satisfied with our conclusion, most [of the lawyers involved in the case] felt it was best for me to stick to the point as I had been making it: Legal rights attach at birth."[81]

That point was the one on which Weddington spent the most time during her allotted half hour. "Your case depends primarily, then, on our holding that the fetus is not a person with constitutional rights," Justice Brennan said to her. "If it were established that the fetus were a life, you would have a difficult case, wouldn't you?" Justice Stewart asked.[82] When Robert Flowers, arguing on behalf of Texas, began his half-hour argument, he first boldly stated that "It is the position of the State of Texas that upon conception we have a human being, a person within the concept of the Constitution of the United States and that of Texas, also."[83] Justice Stewart asked if Flowers considered that question legal, constitutional, or medical. A dialogue proceeded, spinning around the question, which neither the Constitution nor the medical evidence clearly had answered. Flowers's other major point was that a woman's right to privacy should be protected through legislation and not through a Supreme Court ruling.[84] Flowers summed up his stand by calling unborn children a "silent minority" deserving of protection by the state.[85]

Because she reserved four minutes for rebuttal, Sarah Weddington was the last attorney to speak. "We are not here to advocate abortion," she stated solemnly:

> We do not ask this Court to rule that abortion is good, or desirable in any particular situation. We are here to advocate that the decision as to whether or not a particular woman will continue to carry or will terminate a pregnancy is a decision that should be made by that individual, that in fact she has a constitutional right to make that decision for herself, and that the State has shown no interest in [or sufficient legal status to allow] interfering with that decision.[86]

The hearing ended soon after that, and everyone involved went home. Now they would wait for the court's decision in *Roe v. Wade.*

6

The Decision

At 10 a.m. on Monday, January 22, 1973, the Supreme Court released its verdict in the case of *Roe v. Wade.* The news sped over the wires. The Court found in favor of the appellee, Jane Roe. "Our conclusion that Art. 1196 [the Texas statute forbidding abortion] is unconstitutional means, of course, that the Texas abortion statutes, as a unit, must fall," the court decision read.[87] In fact, the decision meant that the laws against abortion in nearly every state in the Union had been deemed unconstitutional and therefore without any holding power.

It had taken more than three months for the court to announce the decision. The process by which Supreme Court justices express their decisions has two parts: the decision, done by structured discussion and a vote among the justices; and the writing of the decision, which is assigned to a single judge. Records published later indicate that the first court, made up of only seven judges, was already inclined to rule in favor of Jane Roe. Harry Blackmun was assigned to write the decision. As Powell and Rehnquist were joining the court and the decision was made to hear rearguments, Blackmun used the time to research the medical literature on the questions involved with conception, fetal development, and abortion. "He was looking for a way," one pair of legal historians believes, "to bring the Court together on the conflicting scientific evidence in the two sides' briefs."[88] Even having done that research, Blackmun composed the final decision slowly. He wanted to find a statement to which the largest number of justices would agree. He circulated several drafts, which the justices considered and responded to by memo. Finally, he finalized the decision for publication. It ran more than 12,000 words long.

To the central document expressing the opinion of the court, justices can append their own statements. A judge may wish to concur with the final decision, yet emphasize a different argument from the one written in the court's statement. Or a judge may have been in the minority, voting against the ultimate decision, and wish to express arguments on the other side. In the case of *Roe v. Wade,* Justice Stewart added a concurring opinion, and Justice Rehnquist wrote a dissenting opinion.

Court decisions are written to a standard format, but within that format, a justice can choose to vary according to his or her interests or concerns and the details of the case in question. The decision on *Roe v. Wade* began, therefore, with a paragraph summarizing the appeal—the lower court decision in Texas and the reasons for reconsidering it—and then listed brief, succinct statements of the holdings found by the court. In the first few pages, in other words, the end result of the court's deliberations were announced. First, the case is appropriate to be heard by the Supreme Court; second, Jane

Telegram
western union

HO. WDS.-CL. OF SVC.	PD. OR COLL.	CASH NO.	CHARGE TO THE ACCOUNT OF	OVER NIGHT TELEGRAM

COLLECT

UNLESS BOX ABOVE IS CHECKED THIS
MESSAGE WILL BE SENT AS A TELEGRAM

Send the following message, subject to the terms on back hereof, which are hereby agreed to

TO   Sarah Weddington

STREET & NO.   Weddington and Weddington
709 West Fourteenth Street
CITY & STATE Austin, Texas

CARE OF   January 22   19 73
OR APT. NO.

TELEPHONE

ZIP CODE 78701

JUDGMENT ROE against WADE today AFFIRMED IN PART AND REVERSED IN

PART JUDGMENT DOE against BOLTON MODIFIED AND AFFIRMED   Opinions

AIRMAILED

SENDER'S TEL. NO. 70-18 Appellants NAME & ADDRESS   Michael Rodak, Jr., Clerk
7D-4h   Supreme Court of United States

Sarah Weddington received a "collect" telegram on January 22, 1973, announcing the Supreme Court's decision in the *Roe v. Wade* case.

Roe has a good reason to sue the state of Texas. Point three summarized the decisions:

> State criminal abortion laws, like those involved here, that except from criminality only a life-saving procedure on the mother's behalf without regard to the stage of her pregnancy and other interests involved violate the Due Process Clause of the Fourteenth Amendment, which protects against state action the right to privacy, including a woman's qualified right to terminate her pregnancy.[89]

The judges added to this point a qualification that granted some state responsibility for both the pregnant woman and the fetus she carries:

"Though the State cannot override that right, it has legitimate interests in protecting both the pregnant woman's
health and the potentiality of human life, each of which
interests grows and reaches a 'compelling' point at various
stages of the woman's approach to term."[90]

To express this sense that the state's responsibility for the
fetus grows over time, Justice Blackmun drew from his research
in the medical literature. He used the concept that pregnancy
could be divided into three stages, or trimesters, as a way to
designate the changing balance between a woman's right to private decision-making and the state's responsibility to protect
all citizens. It was an idea that no attorney, on either side of
the argument, had offered, and for that reason it became a sur-
prising new feature in the legal discussion of abortion rights.
During the first trimester, the Supreme Court decision stated,
"the abortion decision and its effectuation must be left to the
medical judgment of the pregnant woman's attending physician." After the first trimester, the holding allowed state law, "if
it chooses," to "regulate the abortion procedure in ways that are
reasonably related to maternal health." The language gave states
some leeway in such legislation but clearly focused the state's
responsibility on protecting the woman, not the fetus.[91]

The decision further allowed state laws, however, to protect
the fetus in the "stage subsequent to viability." *Viability* was a word
and concept also arising from Blackmun's medical research and
not from either side's argument in the case. A modern equivalent
to the old English legal term quickening, it means the stage when
a fetus could survive outside the mother's body. From that point
on, "the State, in promoting its interest in the potentiality of human life, may, if it chooses, regulate, and even proscribe, abortion
except where necessary, in appropriate medical judgment, for the
preservation of the life or health of the mother." [92]

By dividing a pregnancy into trimesters, the court had
a way to balance the privacy rights of women with the state's

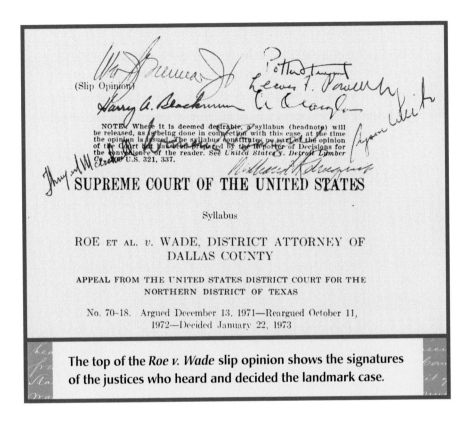

SUPREME COURT OF THE UNITED STATES

Syllabus

ROE ET AL. *v.* WADE, DISTRICT ATTORNEY OF
DALLAS COUNTY

APPEAL FROM THE UNITED STATES DISTRICT COURT FOR THE
NORTHERN DISTRICT OF TEXAS

No. 70-18. Argued December 13, 1971—Reargued October 11,
1972—Decided January 22, 1973

The top of the *Roe v. Wade* slip opinion shows the signatures
of the justices who heard and decided the landmark case.

responsibility for protecting individuals. There was no clear
definition of viability, though, either in the written decision itself
or in the medical profession. Later in the decision, footnoting an
obstetrics textbook, Blackmun wrote, "Viability is usually placed
at about seven months (28 weeks) but may occur earlier, even
at 24 weeks."[93] The fact is, the age of viability differs from one
individual fetus to another. As medical technology advances, the
age at which a fetus can survive changes, too. What appeared in
the *Roe v. Wade* decision to be a clear and objective dividing line
turned out to be a concept wide open to interpretation—and a
springboard for more legal arguments in years to come.

Points four and five, which opened the written decision,
concerned the definition of *physician* and the effect that the
Supreme court decision would have on Texas law enforcement.
First, the court gave states the right to regulate the licensing,

hence the definition, of physician and to forbid abortions provided by any unlicensed practitioner. Second, the court put into writing the understood rule that once a Supreme Court ruling overturns state law, that law no longer stands: "Texas authorities will doubtless fully recognize the Court's ruling that the Texas criminal abortion statutes are unconstitutional."[94]

IN SUPPORT OF THE HOLDING

As in all Supreme Court decisions, the holding in *Roe v. Wade* was accompanied by a measured, logical, and detailed discussion of the issues involved. Justice Blackmun, author of the court decision, began by recognizing "the sensitive and emotional nature of the abortion controversy" and "the deep and seemingly absolute convictions that the subject inspires." Philosophy, experiences, religion, family training, moral values, and standards all enter into each American citizen's response to the abortion issue. "Our task, of course, is to resolve the issue by constitutional measurement, free of emotion and of predilection,"[95] he stated. Personal or public opinion is not to be considered, but rather the rule of law. Blackmun quoted the revered Supreme Court justice, Oliver Wendell Holmes, Jr., who wrote,

> [The U.S. Consitution] is made for people of fundamentally differing views, and the accident of our finding certain opinions natural and familiar or novel and even shocking ought not to conclude our judgment upon the question whether statutes embodying them conflict with the Constitution of the United States.[96]

The court's written decision began with a summary of the Texas law involved and then briefly recorded the stories of Jane Roe, James Hubert Hallford, and John and Mary Doe. One by one, the document outlined the discussion of whether each case warrants a Supreme Court decision. Since both Hallford and the Does sought future relief, it was decided that their cases were not cases to be decided at the federal level. In the case of

Jane Roe, however, the court saw that "she presented a justiciable controversy." Even though she was no longer pregnant at the time of the Supreme Court decision, she was "a pregnant single woman thwarted by the Texas criminal abortion laws" when the case was first brought into court. The law does state that if the controversy no longer exists at the time of appeal, the case is moot, or without standing. But pregnancy presents an exception, the justices decided. A woman is pregnant only 266 days, less than the appeals process itself, and she may become pregnant again. "Our law should not be that rigid," wrote Blackmun. "Pregnancy provides a classic justification for a conclusion of nonmootness."[97]

As an indication of how much the justices reflected on the subject of abortion, Justice Blackmun included a lengthy and scholarly discussion of the history of attitudes and laws

Justice Harry Blackmun, a longtime Republican, was one of the more conservative members of the court. He wrote the majority opinion for *Roe v. Wade*. The *Roe* case was a turning point in Blackmun's career.

about abortion. "It perhaps is not generally appreciated that the restrictive criminal abortion laws in effect in a majority of States today are of relatively recent vintage," stated the decision. Statements and opinions about abortion—from the Persians and the Romans to American laws of the 1950s—show the full array of arguments about the difficult subject. He compared hospital procedures of the nineteenth century to those of the late twentieth century, showing an increase in knowledge, sterile conditions, and technical expertise. To the history, Blackmun added the modern-day positions of the American Medical Association, the American Public Health Association, and the American Bar Association. All three organizations had in recent years published statements recommending the safe, legal, but professionally regulated practice of abortion.

The heart of the legal discussion began with the blunt statement, "The Constitution does not explicitly mention any right of privacy," but then went on to name more than a dozen Supreme Court decisions in which privacy is implied, including *Griswold v. Connecticut,* the decision based on an assumption of a penumbra of rights associated with the Bill of Rights and later constitutional amendments. No matter where it is anchored in the Constitution, wrote Blackmun, the right of privacy "is broad enough to encompass a woman's decision whether or not to terminate her pregnancy." The decision listed all the detriments imposed on the pregnant woman and society were she restricted from choosing abortion: medical harm, distressing future, psychological harm, and decreased mental or physical health. "There is also the distress, for all concerned, associated with the unwanted child," wrote Blackmun, "and there is the problem of bringing a child into a family already unable, psychologically and otherwise, to care for it. . . . All these are factors the woman and her responsible physician necessarily will consider in consultation."[99]

The Supreme Court decision did address the difficult question of whether the fetus was a person in the eyes of U.S. law. By analyzing the language in many prior Supreme Court decisions and in various articles of legislation, the justices determined that "the word 'person,' as used in the Fourteenth Amendment, does not include the unborn." On the other hand, the decision continued, "the pregnant woman cannot be isolated in her privacy." Here the decision specifically referred to an illustrated medical dictionary to demonstrate that "at some point in time another interest . . . becomes significantly involved," and "the woman's privacy is no longer sole and any right of privacy she possesses must be measured accordingly."[100]

The justices were, of course, fully aware that on this point, they were entering the realm of philosophy and religion. "When those trained in the respective disciplines of medicine, philosophy, and theology are unable to arrive at any consensus," wrote the justice, "the judiciary, at this point in the development of man's knowledge, is not in a position to speculate as to the answer." Narrowing the focus simply to law and legal precedent, though, "the unborn have never been recognized in the law as persons in the whole sense." For Texas law to do otherwise is to formulate law based on "one theory of life." A state does, though, "have an important and legitimate interest" in the health of the woman and "still another important and legitimate interest in protecting the potentiality of human life." These are "separate and distinct" interests. "Each grows in substantiality as the woman approaches term and, at a point during pregnancy, each becomes 'compelling'"—a word used by the court to mean a situation in which the state must take responsibility. From this argument, the decision moves quickly to identifying that "point during pregnancy" as the time when the fetus becomes viable, able to survive on its own.[101]

APPENDED OPINIONS

Justice Potter Stewart added a concurring opinion to Justice Blackmun's report of the court's decision. Although he agreed with the final decision, his reasoning was different, so he chose

The most conservative member of the Supreme Court during the *Roe* case, William Rehnquist was most often the sole dissenter of the Burger Court. Controversial throughout his term, Rehnquist was appointed chief justice by President Ronald Reagan in 1986.

to append (attach) a differing opinion. "The Court today is correct in holding that the right asserted by Jane Roe is embraced within the personal liberty protected by the Due Process Clause of the Fourteenth Amendment," wrote Stewart. He did not agree, however, that privacy comes within the penumbra of rights guaranteed by the Constitution. "The protection of a person's general right to privacy—his right to be let alone by other people—is, like the protection of his property and of his very life, left largely to the law of the individual states."[102]

Justice William Rehnquist, new to the court that year, wrote a dissenting opinion. "The Court's opinion brings to the decision of this troubling question both extensive historical fact and a wealth of legal scholarship," he began respectfully. "I find myself nonetheless in fundamental disagreement with those parts of it that invalidate the Texas statute in question."[103] He outlined his reasons. First, the court decision to protect the woman exclusively during the first trimester of pregnancy raised the question of Jane Roe's own state of pregnancy when she brought suit against Texas. In other words, the very question of whether Roe fit the conditions of the decision was unanswered, wrote Rehnquist.

Beyond that detail, though, Rehnquist had more fundamental disagreements with the decision. "I have difficulty in concluding, as the Court does, that the right of 'privacy' is involved in this case," he stated. An abortion procedure is a transaction between parties, hence of concern to the state. Rehnquist questioned the legality of "the Court's sweeping invalidation of any restrictions on abortion during the first trimester" and suggested that such a decision would be "far more appropriate to a legislative judgment than to a judicial one"—in other words, that such rules should be expressed as state laws rather than considered by the Supreme Court.[104]

Rehnquist held existing state law in high regard. State laws dating back a century place restrictions on abortion, and those laws, made by elected legislators, can be assumed to reflect public opinion. "The very existence of the debate is evidence that the 'right' to an abortion is not so universally accepted as the appellant would have us believe," Rehnquist pointed out. In fact, he added, by the time of the Fourteenth Amendment, at least 36 states had enacted abortion limitations. Twenty-one of those pre–Civil War abortion laws had not yet been challenged. "The only conclusion possible from this history," commented Rehnquist, "is that the drafters did not intend to have the Fourteenth Amendment withdraw from the States the power to legislate with respect to this matter"—namely, abortion.[105]

In one last paragraph, Rehnquist pointed out that the Court ruled to strike down the Texas statute entirely, but that in fact the decision of the Court only affected women during the first trimester of pregnancy. Existing Texas law could still apply to women in the second and third trimesters. "For all of the foregoing reasons," concluded Rehnquist, "I respectfully dissent."[106] Many of his arguments would surface again in the years to come.

The Conflicts Continue (1973–1980)

7

The news of the U.S. Supreme Court decision in *Roe v. Wade* was somewhat muffled that day, January 22, 1973, by another significant event that made state and national history: Lyndon Baines Johnson, Texas lawmaker and thirty-sixth president of the United States, had died of a heart attack at the age of 65. Johnson's death grabbed the headlines, but still the implications of the *Roe* decision brought responses from far and wide.

Among those in favor of legal access to abortions, there was great jubilation; among those opposed, there was shock and dismay. In Texas, Governor Dolph Briscoe issued a terse statement requesting the attorney general for an "evaluation of this ruling and for the alternatives open to Texas as a result of the Supreme Court's decision." Lieutenant Governor Bill Hobby stated that same day, "It is in my opinion that the best solution is one in which the state is neutral on the subject of abortion. I believe the medical profession of Texas will respond to the decision and will treat abortion as a medical matter in a responsible way."[107] Austin doctor Fred Hansen performed Texas's first legal abortion for a University of Texas nursing faculty member who had planned to fly to New York for a legal abortion that same day. Sarah Weddington learned of the decision through a phone call to her office from a *New York Times* reporter. She tried to telephone Jane Doe to share the news, but she couldn't reach her.

January 22, 1973, was just another day for Norma McCorvey. Her life had taken a turn for the better, though. She had found the woman of her life. She and Connie Gonzales lived together in the Dallas suburbs. They operated an independent contracting service, N. L. McCorvey & Company. They worked in apartment buildings, cleaning or painting. They worked long hours, and they were starting to get just a little bit ahead. On that Monday, Norma sat at the kitchen table with a beer and the newspaper, while Connie took a shower. She scanned the front page.

McCorvey noticed a small, matter-of-fact article that said that the U.S. Supreme Court had legalized abortion all over the United States. That it was now perfectly okay for a woman to get an abortion in Texas, or anywhere else. That the court had decided seven to two in favor of an anonymous plaintiff in a test case, a challenge to the antiabortion law, called *Roe v. Wade*. The article talked about the attorneys in the case. It talked about the Supreme Court justices—which ones voted for it, which ones against it—but it didn't have anything to say about the plaintiff.

Norma drew in a deep breath. "For a long while I just stared into space, fighting my emotions." When Connie came into the kitchen, McCorvey told her what the article said. Gonzales

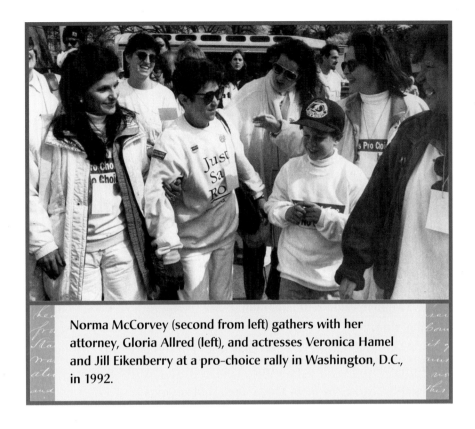

Norma McCorvey (second from left) gathers with her attorney, Gloria Allred (left), and actresses Veronica Hamel and Jill Eikenberry at a pro-choice rally in Washington, D.C., in 1992.

thought it was good news to hear that abortions were now an option for women. "How would you like to meet Jane Roe?" Norma asked her partner. "Oh, Pixie, come on," Connie answered. "We don't know anybody like that."[108] Norma McCorvey had never told her best friend that a Supreme Court battle was going on over something that happened in her own life.

On behalf of the anonymous plaintiff, Sarah Weddington made a public statement:

> I am pleased because of the impact this decision will have on the lives of many women who in the past have suffered because of the current Texas law. I am especially pleased that the decision is a solid seven-to-two decision and that it was based on the right of privacy. I feel very humble to be able to represent the class of women affected by this decision and hope their lives will be the better for it.[109]

Privately, though, Weddington had her worries. She focused closely on the section granting that the overturned Texas law was founded on "one theory of life," and that the Supreme Court recognizes the state's "important and legitimate interest" in the health of the woman and "in protecting the potentiality of human life." She sensed in that language room for reinterpretation. "I knew the opposition would use that to try to put a camel through a keyhole," she wrote later. "I worried that if the medical community came up with similar rules of thumb to apply to abortion, even after we had won our case, medical services might not be as uniformly available as had been our goal."[110] The trimester approach, a surprise to Weddington, seemed to grant to the state and to doctors licensed by the state a great deal of decision-making power over a woman's access to abortion.

Commentators agreed that the Supreme Court ruling would not be the last word. The decision, wrote columnist Jane Brody in the *New York Times,* "left unanswered a number of serious medical and legal questions," even though it would have immediate impact on laws and procedures in every state of the Union.[111] According to New York lawyer Harriet Pilpel, an expert in reproductive law and an outspoken advocate for Planned Parenthood at the time, "Until new laws are passed, doctors can go ahead and perform abortions."[112]

In January 1973, all but four states had restrictive laws that the Supreme Court ruling now deemed unconstitutional. Some legislatures immediately wrote new statutes to fit the new ruling. Others, including Texas, simply let the old laws stand but did not enforce them. A number of representatives, both state and federal, began drafting legislation that fit within the guidelines of the *Roe* decision yet established governmental control at the highest possible level, including physician licensing, site inspections, reporting requirements, advertising bans, rules against public funding, and requirements for informed consent of husbands or parents.[113] In May 1973, seven senators, led by a conservative Republican from New York, James L. Buckley, proposed an amendment to the U.S. Constitution prohibiting all abortions but those to save the life of the pregnant woman. Buckley cited several recent state referenda in which proabortion initiatives had been voted down. He told reporters that "enactment of a constitutional amendment was the only way to reinstate restrictions on abortion."[114] Other congressmen were discussing legislation to counteract the Supreme Court ruling.

Meanwhile, few locales were ready to provide abortions as openly as new laws might allow, and doctors hesitated to open clinics or provide abortion services in hospitals for fear that they might misinterpret shifting law and lay themselves open to prosecution. By and large, abortions still cost well over $100—a significant amount in the early 1970s and certainly more than the average working-class woman could pay. "We must understand that the battle has only just begun," wrote a commentator in Austin's city paper, *The Rag*—the paper on which Sarah Weddington had worked. "An abortion still costs $140, more than many pregnant women can afford; few doctors have the modern equipment; most will still require the consent of a husband."[115] What seemed at first glance a victory was quickly turning into a new set of challenges for those in favor of women's open access to abortions. NARAL—a nationwide organization formed in 1969 and calling itself the National Association for the Repeal of Abortion Laws—reorganized its efforts. It kept the same acronym, but called itself the National Abortion Rights Action League.

A national organization quickly formed on the other side of the issue, as well. In Arizona, cardiologist Carolyn Gerster remembers the day she calls Black Monday. "Once or twice a decade, a catastrophe of such magnitude occurs," Gerster wrote in 2003, "that every person recalls precisely where they were when the news broke. So it was with *Roe v. Wade*." She had just arrived at her office. She was parking her car. The radio was on. The program was interrupted. "Most of us in Arizona," she wrote,

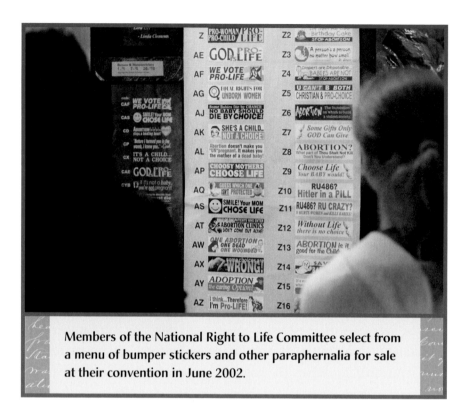

Members of the National Right to Life Committee select from a menu of bumper stickers and other paraphernalia for sale at their convention in June 2002.

"were frozen by despair and disbelief." A proposal quickly surfaced among those who shared deep convictions against the practice of abortion. "We must regroup, as the abolitionists had over a century before," wrote Gerster of those times. "A national organization was required."[116]

A planning group began meeting monthly, each one flying in to Chicago's O'Hare Airport, as Gerster described it:

People of different backgrounds, united for one purpose: the establishment of a national organization to engage in educational, charitable, scientific, and political activity to promote respect for the worth and dignity of all human life, including the life of the unborn child from the moment of conception, and to promote, encourage, and sponsor such amendatory and statutory measures which would provide protection of human life before and after birth, particularly for the defenseless, the incompetent, the impaired, and the incapacitated.[117]

The National Right to Life Committee (NRLC) was incorporated as a nonprofit organization in March 1973. In June 1973, 800 people gathered in Detroit for the first NRLC convention, stating that they considered the Supreme Court decision an "irresponsible exercise of raw judicial powers." They adopted a resolution affirming that "all prolife supporters throughout this country are mandated to seek out and encourage their U.S. Congressmen and Senators to sponsor, co-sponsor or publicly endorse" a "mandatory human amendment" of the sort proposed by Senator Buckley.[118]

If anything, the battle had become more bitter by the first anniversary of the *Roe v. Wade* decision. Competing demonstrations took place in major cities across the country on January 22, 1974. In Washington, D.C., 6,000 people protesting against abortion rallied together, cheering Buckley and listening to others promise to enact legislation or constitutional amendments limiting or banning abortion. In New York, members of a group called Catholics for Free Choice staged a mock ceremony, crowning a woman pope on the steps of St. Patrick's Cathedral and implying that edicts against abortion arose from the church's male-dominated power structure.

BATTLE LINES DRAWN

Although newspaper reporters still used the terms *proabortionists* and *antiabortionists*, the rhetoric of the debate was settling on two highly charged labels to name the opposing positions. Those attempting to undo the legalized abortion rules called themselves *prolife*, referring to their beliefs that life begins just after conception, and that therefore the fetus is a human life deserving of protection from the first weeks of pregnancy on. That term might imply that anyone against their position was against life. Abortion advocates quickly countered by calling themselves *prochoice*, emphasizing that they were not advocating abortion itself but women's right to choose it.

In April 1974, news from Boston showed the nation that the Supreme Court decision in *Roe v. Wade* by no means put an end to the prosecution of doctors performing abortions. Kenneth Edelin—a highly respected physician and chief resident for obstetrics and gynecology at Boston City Hospital—was indicted after performing an abortion on a woman 24 weeks into her pregnancy. The case brought against Edelin tested the definition of viability so central to the *Roe* decision. Boston's district attorney charged that the fetus he removed had in fact

 RELIGION AND ABORTION

Abortion issues involve powerful and baffling questions. When does life begin? What rights do humans have to manipulate life? Many would say that the answers to these questions should come from churches, synagogues, and mosques, not the courts or the legislature.

Church laws and religious leaders have influenced the debate over abortion for centuries. The laws of the Catholic Church, called "canon law," influenced the early English legal system. Prevailing Protestant religions and their moral codes shaped early American laws on abortion as well. When the abortion debates reentered the public arena in the 1970s, religious leaders spoke up loud and clear—on both sides of the argument.

Catholic canon law today equates abortion with homicide. Both result in excommunication, or an end to church membership. Conservative branches of Protestant denominations oppose abortion as well. These groups include the Southern Baptist Convention, the African Methodist Episcopal (AME) Church, the Church of Jesus Christ of the Latter-day Saints (the Mormons), and Eastern Orthodox churches. Local or unaffiliated churches that could be called charismatic, pentecostal, or been viable, capable of living on its own, and so Edelin's act was not abortion but manslaughter.[119] The doctor was convicted of manslaughter in February 1975, but Massachusetts's Supreme Court overturned that decision nearly two years later.

A number of lawsuits over abortion rights reached the U.S. Supreme Court in the years immediately after *Roe v. Wade*. In *Planned Parenthood of Central Missouri v. Danforth* (1976), the Court declared unconstitutional the Missouri law that required that the husband of a woman give consent before her abortion is provided. In *Bellotti v. Baird* (1979), the court limited the states' rights to require parental consent before an abortion for

fundamentalist share the same ethical stance. Some of the more conservative groups may consider abortion ethical if it is necessary to save the life of the woman.

A number of religious denominations express support for broader access to abortion, however. More than 8 out of 10 Jews in the United States consider themselves prochoice.* Leaders from a number of Protestant denominations—American Baptist (USA), Episcopal (USA), Presbyterian (USA), Unitarian Universalist, United Methodist, and United Church of Christ—support keeping abortion a legal option, a private choice for the woman and her doctor.

Whereas religious spokespeople disagree on the law of the land, they do agree on one principle: Abortion is never the preferred response to any woman's pregnancy.**

---

*Religious Institute on Sexual Morality, Justice, and Healing, "An Open Letter to Religious Leaders on Abortion as a Moral Decision," http://www.religiousinstitute.org.

**Information from Ontario Consultants on Religious Tolerance, http://www.religioustolerance.org.

a woman under 18 years old. Several cases raised the issue of using state or federal welfare funds to pay for abortions. Congress amended a spending bill in 1976 and forbade the use of Medicaid and other welfare funds on abortions, allowing for exceptions in the cases of rape, incest, health risks, or danger of death to the mother. A suit questioning that legislation reached the Supreme Court in 1980, and the court affirmed that the law was constitutional.

In 1981, the Hyde Amendment—named for U.S. Representative Henry J. Hyde of Illinois, who originally proposed it—was reworded by the legislature to keep public funds from paying for any abortions other than those "where the life of the mother would be endangered if the fetus were carried to term."[120] Many argued against the restriction, stating that it effectively removed abortion as an option for millions of American women who depended on Medicaid to cover healthcare costs. The arguments continued, and in 1993, the amendment changed again to the wording that still stands today, allowing Medicaid and other federal welfare funds to go toward abortions only in the cases of rape, incest, or threat of death to the mother:

> None of the funds appropriated under this Act [the Health and Human Services/Education appropriations bill] shall be expended for any abortion except when it is made known to the federal entity or official to which funds are appropriated under this Act that such procedure is necessary to save the life of the mother or that the pregnancy is the result of an act or rape or incest.[121]

Whereas the Hyde Amendment controls federal welfare spending, more than a dozen states developed their own welfare plans and provide state support for indigent women seeking abortions.[122]

In the courts, in the legislatures, in the lecture halls, and on the street, arguments about abortion seethed and boiled over. It became a campaign issue, a rallying point for liberals

The Hyde Amendment was named after the congressman who originally proposed it, Henry J. Hyde.

and conservatives. Amid advances in medical science, new controversies were surfacing that also involved life-and-death ethics: contraception, cloning and genetic engineering, reproductive technologies, euthanasia, and assisted suicide. Abortion became a touchstone topic that stood for them all. Abortion issues mattered during election campaigns in 1980. Campaigns for seats in the U.S. Senate and House also involved debates over abortion, and in 13 out of the 16 races in which abortion was debated, antiabortionists won.[98] Incumbent President Jimmy Carter, running on a pro-choice platform, lost

The hot debate over abortion rights continued in the years after the *Roe* decision. Antiabortion Governor Ronald Reagan defeated pro-choice President Jimmy Carter in the 1980 presidential election.

to Ronald Reagan, a former actor and popular past governor of California.

Ironically, it was under Governor Reagan that California had passed liberal abortion laws in the 1960s, making it, along with New York, the state to which women all over the country traveled for an abortion. Within a year, though, Reagan admitted that he had made a mistake, and by the time he ran for president, he spoke out vehemently against legalized abortion. The 1980 Republican Party Platform—the written statement of the principles represented by Reagan as the Republican candidate for president—clearly stated support for "a constitutional amendment to restore protection of the right to life for unborn children" and for "Congressional efforts to restrict the use of taxpayers' dollars for abortion."[124] It also directly attacked recent Supreme Court decisions about parent consent, saying, "We protest the Supreme Court's intrusion into the family structure through its denial of the parent's obligation and right to guide their minor children."[125] Such statements linked to another platform theme, the preference of family over government as the source of guiding rules. "Unlike the Democrats," the platform statement read, "we do not advocate new federal bureaucracies with ominous power to shape a national family order. Rather, we insist that all domestic policies, from child care and schooling to Social Security and the tax code, must be formulated with the family in mind."[126]

Compared with the Republic platform—which represented campaign strategy—the Democratic Party Platform of 1980 deemphasized both abortion and family. "We fully recognize the religious and ethical concerns which many Americans have about abortion," read the document. "We also recognize the belief of many Americans that a woman has a right to choose whether and when to have a child." The platform asserted support for the Supreme Court decision in *Roe v. Wade* "as the law of the land" and specifically opposed "any constitutional amendment to restrict or overturn that decision."[127] That year, Ronald Reagan won by a landslide. Prolife activists considered it their victory.

EQUAL·JUSTICE·UNDER·LAW·

8

The Future of
Roe v. Wade

With each new Supreme Court hearing related to *Roe v. Wade*, advocates for and against legalized abortion paid close attention to the way each justice cast a vote. There was a sense that among the justices, as among the general public, private beliefs would influence their response to abortion issues. In *Roe*, seven justices decided in favor of broadened access to abortion, and two voted against it. In several abortion cases coming before the court soon after *Roe*, Chief Justice Warren Burger seemed to switch sides. Many decisions on abortion cases were decided by a 6 to 3 vote, and the balance was tipping. A case testing the constitutionality of the Hyde Amendment in

1980 brought a decision of five to four in favor of the legislative ban on using Medicaid funds to pay for abortions other than those that would save the woman's life.

Hopes were mixed, but spirits were high when President Ronald Reagan nominated Sandra Day O'Connor to fill the spot vacated as Justice Potter Stewart retired. If approved, O'Connor would be the first woman to serve on the Supreme Court. As with all Supreme Court nominees, O'Connor had to be approved by the Senate Judiciary Committee. Committee members studied her career record and interviewed her intensely. She was confirmed by all but one member of the Senate Judiciary Committee. Jesse Helms of North Carolina declined to vote, objecting to O'Connor's answers about *Roe v. Wade*.

Senator Strom Thurmond, chairman of the committee, asked her directly about her personal and judicial philosophy on abortion. O'Connor began by stating that a judge's "personal views and philosophies . . . should be set aside insofar as it is possible to do that in resolving matters that come before the Court." She continued, "My own view in the area of abortion is that I am opposed to it as a matter of birth control or otherwise," adding that "the subject of abortion is a valid one, in my opinion, for legislative action subject to any constitutional restraints or limitations." Questioned on several votes she had cast while a senator in her home state of Arizona, O'Connor made it clear that her personal beliefs did not necessarily drive her decisions. She had, for example, co-sponsored a bill to provide family planning services. Senator Thurmond characterized it as a bill supporting "surgical procedures, even for minors without parental consent." O'Connor responded, "I supported the availability of contraceptive information to the public generally. . . . It seemed to me that perhaps the best way to avoid having people who were seeking abortions was to enable people not to become pregnant unwittingly or without the intention of doing so." When asked of her vote in 1974 against a bill urging Congress to pass a constitutional amendment against abortion, O'Connor

The first woman to serve on the U.S. Supreme Court, Sandra Day O'Connor was seen as a beacon of hope by many American women. During her interviews with the Senate Judiciary Committee, O'Connor stated that her legal opinions and her personal beliefs about abortion might not always match.

answered that she considered the bill to have been too hastily written. "Amendments to the Constitution are very serious matters," she continued, "and should be undertaken after a great deal of study and thought . . . I did not feel at that time that that kind of consideration had been given to the measure."[128]

O'Connor's unwillingness to talk about the way she would vote on abortion cases became the focal point of her nomination hearings. Three senators on the committee, all adamantly opposed to legal abortion, felt frustrated by her refusal. One consulted with antiabortion activists in Arizona, who assured him that despite her silence, she supported their cause. Another trusted that if President Reagan nominated her, her decisions would lean in his favored direction. Two of the senators finally cast votes in favor of O'Connor's nomination, but the third, Jeremiah Denton, a Republican from Alabama, abstained. From a committee of 18 members, she received 17 votes in favor, 0 against, and 1 abstention.[129] The Senate confirmed her nomination, and on September 26, 1981, Sandra Day O'Connor became the first female U.S. Supreme Court justice. And as it turned out, she did make history in the national conversation about abortion law.

THE CONCEPT OF UNDUE BURDEN

In the 10 years after the *Roe v. Wade* decision, numerous state and local laws were passed, placing greater restrictions and rules about abortion on women seeking them, doctors performing them, and clinics and hospitals providing the service. Three cases questioning such rules reached the U.S. Supreme Court in 1983. A Virginia doctor had performed a late-term abortion in a facility that had not been licensed by the state. Missouri had passed laws requiring a second physician at late-term abortions, to determine fetal viability; requiring minors to get consent either from parents or a juvenile court judge; and allowing only hospitals, not local clinics, to perform medically necessary late-term abortions. Akron, Ohio, had passed restrictions on the practice of abortion in all the city's hospitals. The Akron City Council's resolutions began by stating that "there is no point in time between the union of the sperm and egg . . . and the birth of the infant at which point we can say the unborn child is not a human life."[130] In every case, those charged appealed their cases, claiming them to contradict the Supreme Court's decision in *Roe v. Wade*.

The court supported the conviction of the Virginia doctor. It allowed Missouri's regulations, except the one limiting clinic practice. In the Akron case, the court considered an amicus brief submitted by Rex Lee, the U.S. solicitor general—the attorney representing the U.S. government. Lee was given 10 minutes to speak. He argued against the trimester-based principles at the heart of the *Roe* decision and presented instead a concept he had heard in several previous decisions. When the Supreme Court had agreed that welfare money should not go to pay for abortions, the justices had written that a regulation limiting abortion "is not unconstitutional unless it unduly burdens the right to seek an abortion." Solicitor General Lee encouraged the court to use this rule, rather than the trimester concept, as a way to judge all abortion cases. The suggestion infuriated Justice Blackmun, author of the *Roe* decision and originator of the trimester rule.[131]

Although the court ruled six to three against the City of Akron, Justice O'Connor wrote the dissenting opinion and discussed the concept of undue burden. "In my view," she wrote, "this 'unduly burdensome' standard should be applied to the challenged regulations throughout the entire pregnancy without reference to the particular 'stage' of pregnancy involved." The court's job should be to decide if a local or state regulation, in other words, does not "unduly burden" or seriously limit a citizen's rights, but not to "strike down laws because they do not meet our standards of desirable social policy, 'wisdom,' or 'common sense.'"[132] With the introduction of the principle of undue burden, the trimester rule at the heart of *Roe v. Wade* rule lost its power. The next two important Supreme Court decisions on abortion matters followed the trend.

Despite the previous decision, the Missouri legislature continued to apply complicated rules to the practice of abortions. A new case questioned the law. Coming before the Supreme Court in 1989 as *Webster v. Reproductive Health Services*, doctors and nurses at a public hospital and at St. Louis's oldest abortion clinic challenged William L. Webster, attorney general of Missouri, stating that the rules were unconstitutional. Demonstrators on both sides, prolife and prochoice, clamored outside the court building the morning that arguments were presented. There were several points of discussion. The law began with a preamble stating that the "life of each human being begins at conception," but the justices found that the preamble was too abstract to deny the rights of a person in practice.[133] The law required that from the seventeenth week of pregnancy on, abortions must occur in hospitals, but also that no public hospitals or public hospital workers could perform abortions, following previous rulings that supported limits to publicly funded abortions. Doctors in Missouri were forbidden to suggest abortion to a patient and, if the patient asked, could only read language about abortion provided by the legislature. Finally, before performing an abortion, doctors had to perform three tests to determine if the fetus was viable.

Addressing the Supreme Court, Attorney General Webster used the argument that not one of the rules unduly burdened the rights of women as protected under *Roe.* If the justices found that they did, however, he urged the court to overturn *Roe.* In essence, as one history of abortion law phrases it, "The state was asking the Court to allow the state's rules under *Roe* or to throw out *Roe.*"[134] Justice Antonin Scalia, appointed to the court in 1986 by President Reagan, engaged in a dialogue with Frank Susman, the plaintiffs' attorney, that captured the essence of the national debate. Scalia agreed with Susman on the physiological signs that signified viability, but he asked, "What conclusion does that lead you to?"[135] A leap of logic, or faith, went from the observable signs to a legal pronouncement about what they signify. Susman responded,

> When you have an issue that is so divisive and so emotional and so personal, and so intimate, it must be left as a fundamental right to the individual to make that choice. . . . The

very debate that went on outside this morning, outside this building, and has gone on in various towns and communities across our nation is the same debate that every woman who becomes pregnant and doesn't wish to be pregnant has with herself.[136]

The case caused bitter arguments among the justices, the record later showed. Chief Justice Rehnquist, who had voted in the minority on all abortion decisions since he joined the court, staunchly supported the state on all points. Justice O'Connor sought a middle ground, as she believed she had found in the principle of undue burden. Justice Scalia considered abortion rules to be legislative and not judicial matters. Justice Blackmun watched the others dismantling his 1973 decision and accused them of disregarding the law and the rule of *stare decisis* (Latin for "to stand by that which is decided"). By a vote of 5 to 4, the Supreme Court upheld the Missouri laws exerting limits and regulations on the practice of abortion. In the view of Kathryn Kolbert, a reproductive rights attorney, the *Webster* decision "emboldened those who wanted to push the question."[37]

Planned Parenthood v. Casey, a 1992 decision, explicitly abandoned the first-trimester rule in favor of undue burden as a test for the constitutionality of abortion practices. The Court supported Pennsylvania's law that a pregnant woman receive state-scripted literature discouraging abortion and reconsider for 24 hours. More cases rose to the level of the Supreme Court in the coming years, each one weakening *Roe v. Wade* as a solid legal precedent. Observers into the early years of the twenty-first century expected to hear the 1973 decision overturned altogether, although, in all of U.S. history, rarely had the Supreme Court overturned one of its own decisions.

DECADES LATER

As the years went by, the anniversary of the Supreme Court decision in *Roe v. Wade* became an occasion for demonstrations and protests, memories and marches, speeches and rhetoric, especially in Washington, D.C. In the 1970s, when the decision was handed out, the protesters tended to be women, young and old, demanding their rights and crying out in favor of legalized abortion. In the 1990s, as the decision passed its second decade, more often it was the antiabortionists who filled the streets. An estimated 75,000 prolife advocates marched a mile up Constitution Avenue on January 22, 1990. President George W. Bush addressed the crowd by telephone, telling them that he was on their side.[138] On the decision's twentieth anniversary, a *Washington Post* headline termed the conflicts over abortion "America's Longest War."[139]

That war had taken on new dimensions in the early 1990s, as some antiabortion activists turned violent. For years, those objecting to abortion had organized demonstrations and vigils outside clinics across the country. As early as 1976, activists had inflicted physical damage to the buildings, including vandalism, arson, and bombings. Many were arrested, tried, and convicted for such tactics. Most publicly defended their behavior, calling themselves the saviors of the unborn children dying with every abortion. In March 1993, a man stepped out from among those praying in front of the Pensacola, Florida, Women's Medical Services clinic and shot physician David Gunn three times in the back. Some say he cried out, "Don't kill any more babies," just before he pulled the trigger. The gunman, Michael Griffin, surrendered peacefully to police on the scene. He was ultimately sentenced to life in prison for murder.[140]

Investigations revealed that Gunn, who operated an abortion clinic in a nearby Alabama town as well, had been receiving death threats for years. The Christian-based antiabortion group Operation Rescue, perhaps the best known for its clinic demonstrations, decried the murder. "Our commitment to the dignity of life stands for the born as well as the unborn," stated the executive director. Griffin's was the first of a string of violent

Paul Hill was convicted for murdering a doctor and his escort outside a Florida abortion clinic. Considered a hero by many other antiabortion activists, Hill was executed by lethal injection.

attacks at abortion clinics, however. Antiabortionist Paul Hill wrote in 2003,

> Two days after Michael Griffin killed Dr. Gunn, I called the *Phil Donahue Show* [a television talk show] and told them I supported the shooting. . . . Three days later, I appeared on the show with the abortionist's son, and compared killing Dr. Gunn to killing a Nazi concentration camp 'doctor.' . . . [Later] I appeared on ABC's *Nightline,* and justified Shelley Shannon's shooting of an abortionist in Wichita, Kansas, in August 1993.[141]

Hill himself spent countless hours standing outside the very Pensacola clinic where Gunn once practiced, holding pickets with messages like "Execute Murderers—Abortionists." On July 29, 1994, he shot three people: John Britton, the doctor who replaced Gunn at the clinic; Britton's volunteer escort; and the escort's wife. Britton and his escort died. Nine years later, Paul Hill was executed for murder in a Florida state prison. A Web site maintained by his supporters still defends his actions, saying that he was "a well known advocate of the duty to defend both born and unborn children with whatever force is necessary."[142]

At the same time that violence threatened abortion clinics and the doctors practicing in them, medical technology presented two new developments that made the arguments all the more complex: the so-called partial-birth abortion technique and stem cell research.

The public calls it "partial-birth abortion," but the physicians who developed the procedure in the 1980s called it "dilation and extraction" and considered it a safer way to perform an abortion when the fetus is 20 to 26 weeks old. Drugs dilate the woman's cervix, then the fetus is removed, legs first. The contents of the fetal skull are drained to release the body fully from the uterus. The procedure represents less than one percent of all abortions, but it has gained significant attention from the public and legislators. In 2000, a Nebraska law against all partial-birth abortions came before the Supreme Court, which declared it unconstitutional, since it placed an undue burden on a woman who might need a late-term abortion to save her health or life. In a historic move, Congress trumped the Supreme Court finding by passing an act declaring partial-birth abortion "a gruesome and inhuman procedure that is never medically necessary and should be prohibited." Recognizing the implications of this move, the Senate added a statement to the act, affirming *Roe v. Wade* as a decision that was "appropriate," that "secures an important constitutional right," and that "should not be overturned."[143] Nevertheless, the U.S. Congress stepped in where the U.S. Supreme Court had not yet treaded.

Not quite so central, but equally contentious, the new science of stem cell research has become a context for arguments about abortion, as well. Embryonic stem cells—cells produced naturally at a very early stage in embryonic development— hold great promise as the raw material for effective treatments for debilitating diseases, including multiple sclerosis, heart disease, and spinal cord injuries. These remarkable cells can be harvested from embryos developed in laboratories or from tissue from fetuses expelled at eight weeks of gestation or later.[144] Those who object on moral grounds to abortion want

 WHAT EVER HAPPENED TO JANE ROE?

For years after the Supreme Court decision, Norma McCorvey stayed anonymous. In 1989, she agreed to participate in a nationwide pro-choice rally and took one step toward going public. Two days before the rally, a drive-by sniper fired into the house she shared with her partner, Connie Gonzalez. She went to Washington, DC, anyway. She stood on the VIP platform with Jane Fonda and Betty Friedan, even though no one knew her. Gaining in courage, she publicly identified herself as Jane Roe. She started giving speeches, going everywhere from women's clubs all the way to *Good Morning America*. She dedicated life and soul to the prochoice cause.

Putting beliefs into action, McCorvey volunteered at a North Dallas abortion clinic. Like many clinics in the early 1990s, hers was picketed constantly, sometimes by members of Operation Rescue, one of the more visible Christian antiabortion organizations. She got to know the members of Operation Rescue, which opened an office next door to to curb this practice. Efforts to regulate embryonic stem cell research are under way at both the state and the federal levels.

Despite the politics, the demonstrations, and the public outcry, abortions still continue to occur in the United States at one of the highest rates in the world. According to the Guttmacher Institute, half of all American women who find themselves pregnant and do not want a child still choose abortion. Roughly 1.3 million abortions take place in the United States every year. Of those, 88 percent occur within the first 12 weeks of pregnancy, and 55 percent are provided to women age 25 or under. Institute analysts figure that these numbers suggest that at this rate, about one in three American women will have had an abortion by the age of 45. "The United States has one

the clinic. She befriended seven-year-old Emily, the daughter of a picketer. Then she learned that Emily's mother had almost had an abortion. Abortion was no longer an abstraction to McCorvey; it had a face.

Emily and her family invited McCorvey to church. She had never felt appreciated by the prochoice movement, she realized. She was alienated from her lawyer, Sarah Weddington, and had not even been included in the White House *Roe v. Wade* twenty-fifth anniversary. On the other hand, Emily, her parents, other Operation Rescue members—even the pastor, their church, and the God they believed—all embraced her. In 1995, Norma McCorvey experienced an emotional and life-transforming conversion to Christianity and publicly announced her opposition to abortion. She now heads a nonprofit foundation, Roe No More Ministry, that crusades against abortion and supports crisis pregnancy centers that counsel pregnant women without advising abortion.

The most famous symbol of abortion rights in America, Norma McCorvey changed her views in 1995. She is now an advocate for the anti-abortion movement and even petitioned the Supreme Court in 2005 to overturn the landmark *Roe v. Wade* decision.

of the highest abortion rates in the developed world," says one institute expert. "Women from every socioeconomic, racial, ethnic, religious and age group [are] obtaining abortions."[145] The number of abortions provided to American women has dropped slightly since the 1980s, and the number of abortion providers declined 11 percent between 1996 and 2000. Some cheer that their message is convincing doctors and women to turn away from abortion. Others worry that laws and public opinion are sending women to back alleys again. Every time new justices are appointed to the Supreme Court, the press, the public, and the legislators scrutinize their records and rhetoric on abortion cases, considering it a key symbol of the direction in which the law of the nation is moving. America's longest war is still not over.

Chronology

1803 Lord Ellenborough's Act enacted; it is
      first recorded English law against abortion.

1812 First American abortion case is brought to
      trial, in Massachusetts.

1821 First American state law against abortion is
      enacted, in Connecticut.

Timeline

1965
Griswold v. Connecticut, Supreme Court allows Connecticut abortion clinic to operate.

1969
California v. Belous, conviction of abortion doctor is overturned.

June 1970
Judges support *Roe's* claim that Texas abortion laws are unconstitional but do not call for end to further enforcement of laws.

1965   **1971**

May 1970
Case of *Jane Roe v. Henry Wade,* Dallas district attorney, is argued in District Court in Dallas, Texas.

December 1971
Roe v. Wade is argued before U.S. Supreme Court.

1969
NARAL is founded.

108

1828   New York passes law against abortion but allows therapeutic exception to save the life of the woman.

1916   First American birth control clinic in United States is opened in New York City by Margaret Sanger.

1921   Sanger founds American Birth Control League, which eventually becomes Planned Parenthood.

June 1961   In *Poe v. Ullman*, U.S. Supreme Court dismisses appeal questioning Pennsylvania law against doctors prescribing contraceptives to married couples.

June 1972
Court orders reargument of *Roe v. Wade*.

October 1972
Roe v. Wade is reargued before U.S. Supreme Court.

October 1976
Congressional amendment bans use of federal welfare funds for abortions.

1989
In *Webster v. Reproductive Health Services*, Missouri laws limiting abortion access and practice are upheld.

1972

2003

January 1973
U.S. Supreme Court finds for Roe and declares Texas abortion laws unconstitutional. Trimester rule on abortion access is stated.

1983
In three abortion cases, U.S. Supreme Court moves away from trimester rule to undue burden rule.

2003
Congress passes partial-birth abortion ban.

June 1965	In *Griswold v. Connecticut*, U.S. Supreme Court overturns convictions of operators of Planned Parenthood League of Connecticut.
1969	National Association for the Repeal of Abortions Laws is founded.
September 1969	In *California v. Belous*, U.S. Supreme Court overturns conviction of Dr. Leon Belous, accused of providing abortions.
March 3, 1970	Legal counsel for Jane Roe files suit in Texas court.
May 22, 1970	Dallas District Court considers arguments in Jane Roe's case in Austin, Texas.
June 17, 1970	In *Roe v. Wade*, court finds Texas law against abortion unconstitutional but does not order law enforcement officials to stop prosecuting; Weddington begins to plan appeal.
December 13, 1971	*Roe v. Wade* is argued before U.S. Supreme Court.
June 1972	U.S. Supreme Court orders reargument of *Roe v. Wade*.
September 15, 1972	Attorneys submit legal briefs for reargument.
October 11, 1972	*Roe v. Wade* is argued again before U.S. Supreme Court.
January 22, 1973	In *Roe v. Wade*, U.S. Supreme Court finds Texas laws prohibiting abortion to be unconstitutional.
June 1973	First Right to Life convention meets, in Detroit.
February 1975	Boston physician Kenneth Edelin is convicted of manslaughter for performing abortions; ultimately he is cleared of charges.

July 1976   In *Planned Parenthood of Central Missouri v. Danforth*, U.S. Supreme Court allows Missouri law requiring third-party consent for abortions.

October 1976   Congress passes the Hyde Amendment, forbidding the use of federal welfare funds to provide abortions.

September 25, 1981   Sandra Day O'Connor is confirmed as first woman justice of the U.S. Supreme Court.

1983   In three Supreme Court decisions, O'Connor promotes concept of undue burden as test for constitutionality of abortion laws.

July 1989   In *Webster v. Reproductive Health Services*, U.S. Supreme Court upholds numerous Missouri regulations restricting abortion access and practice.

January 22, 1990   On seventeenth anniversary of *Roe v. Wade* decision, 75,000 march in Washington, D.C., against abortion.

June 1992   In *Planned Parenthood v. Casey*, the U.S. Supreme Court upholds Pennsylvania rules on abortion and comes close to overturning *Roe v. Wade* ruling.

March 1993   Dr. David Gunn, a physician providing abortions in Florida, is shot and killed by antiabortion activist Michael Griffin.

July 1993   Dr. John Britton, a physician providing abortions in Florida, is shot and killed by antiabortion activist Paul Hill.

November 5, 2003   President George W. Bush signs into law a partial-birth abortion ban, barring practice of the rare late-term surgical procedure.

Notes

Chapter 1

1. Norma McCorvey with Andy Meisler, *I Am Roe: My Life, Roe v. Wade, and Freedom of Choice* (New York: HarperCollins, 1994, p. 104).
2. Ibid., p. 101.
3. Ibid., p. 11.
4. Ibid., p. 16.
5. Ibid., pp. 15–16.
6. Ibid., p. 27.
7. Ibid., p. 39.
8. Ibid., p. 40.
9. Ibid., p. 41.
10. Ibid., p. 45.
11. Ibid., p. 46.
12. Ibid., p. 47.
13. Ibid., p. 52.
14. Ibid., p. 53.
15. Ibid., p. 70.
16. Ibid., p. 101.
17. Ibid., pp. 114–115.
18. Ibid., p. 113.
19. Ibid.

Chapter 2

20. Exodus 21:22–25, *The New Oxford Annotated Bible,* New Revised Standard Edition (New York: Oxford University Press, 1994).
21. Plato, *Republic,* V, 461c, from Edith Hamilton and Huntington Cairns, eds., *The Collected Dialogues of Plato* (Princeton, NJ: Princeton University Press, 1961, p. 700).
22. Translation from the Greek by Ludwig Edelstein, from his book, *The Hippocratic Oath: Text, Translation, and Interpretation.* Baltimore: Johns Hopkins University Press, 1943. Posted as "Hippocratic Oath—Classical Version," *NOVA Online,* http://www.pbs.org/wgbh/nova/doctors/oath_classical.html/.
23. More details on modern versions of the Hippocratic Oath can be found on the *NOVA Online* Web site, http://www.pbs.org/wgbh/nova/doctors/oath_today.html/.
24. As quoted from the 1855 translation in Mark S. Scott, "Quickening in the Common Law: The Legal Precedent *Roe* Attempted and Failed to Use (note)" (*Michigan Law & Policy Review* 1996: p. 199).
25. As quoted in Mark S. Scott, "Quickening in the Common Law" (note).
26. Ibid., p. 224.
27. Ibid.
28. Ibid., p. 232.
29. *Roe v. Wade,* 410 U.S. 113 (1973).
30. Lord Ellenborough's Act 43 Geo. 3, C. 58 .
31. Ibid.

32. N.E.H. Hull, and Peter Charles Hoffer, *Roe v. Wade: The Abortion Rights Controversy in American History* (Lawrence: University Press of Kansas, 2001, p. 20).

33. Hull and Hoffer, *Roe v. Wade*, p. 21.

34. Quoted in Hull and Hoffer, *Roe v. Wade*, p. 28.

Chapter 3

35. Ibid., p. 64.

36. Ibid., p. 64.

37. Ibid., p. 67.

38. 315 Mass. 394, *Commonwealth v. Daniel R. Wheeler* (1944).

39. As stated by Rev. James Pike, quoted in Hull and Hoffer, *Roe v. Wade*, p. 76.

40. *Poe v. Ullman*, 367 U.S. 497 (1961).

41. Ibid.

42. *Griswold v. Connecticut*, 381 U.S. 479 (1965).

43. Ibid.

44. Ibid.

45. *The People v. Leon Phillip Belous*, 71 Cal.2d 954, 80 Cal.Rptr. 354 (1969).

46. Ibid.

47. Ibid.

48. Ibid.

Chapter 4

49. Sarah Weddington, *A Question of Choice*. New York: Penguin Books, 1993, p. 13.

50. Weddington, *A Question of Choice*, p. 14.

51. Ibid., p. 39.

52. *Girswold v. Connecticut*, 381 U.S. 479 (1965).

53. *Olmstead v. United States*, 277 U.S. 438, 478 (1928).

54. Weddington, *A Question of Choice*, pp. 45–46.

55. Ibid., p. 53.

56. Ibid., p. 54.

57. Ibid., p. 63.

58. Ibid.

59. Ibid., p. 64.

60. Ibid., p. 67.

61. "3 U.S. Judges Rule Laws on Abortion Invalid in Texas," *New York Times*, June 18, 1970, p. 37.

62. Weddington, *A Question of Choice*, pp. 69–70.

Chapter 5

63. July 28, 1970, p. 31.

64. John Sibley, "69,000 Abortions in 6 Months Here," *New York Times* (February 7, 1971): pp. 70.

65. Susan Edmiston, "A Report on the Abortion Capital of the Country," *New York Times Sunday Magazine*, April 11, 1971,: p. 10.

66. "Abortion Law Protest in Paris," *New York Times*, April 5, 1971, p. 28.

67. Paul Hofmann, "Pope Denounces Legal Abortions," *New York Times*, October 13, 1970, p. 2.

68. Marvine Howe, "Vatican Denounces Italian Senate Bill Legalizing Abortion," *New York Times*, August 10, 1971, p. 7.

69. Nathan Lewin, "There Is No Mistaking the Swing of the Pendulum," *New York Times*, June 27, 1971, p. E8.

70. "Nixon Abortion Statement," *New York Times*, April 4, 1971, p. 28.

71. Weddington, *A Question of Choice*, p. 82.
72. Ibid., p. 97.
73. Ibid., p. 99.
74. Hull and Hoffer, *Roe v. Wade*, pp. 146–147.
75. McCorvey, *I Am Roe*, p. 127.
76. Ibid., p. 143.
77. Ibid., p. 127.
78. Hull and Hoffer, *Roe v. Wade*, p. 159.
79. Weddington, *A Question of Choice*, p. 120; Hull and Hoffer, *Roe v. Wade*, p. 159.
80. Weddington, *A Question of Choice*, p. 131.
81. Ibid., p. 137.
82. Ibid., pp. 138–139.
83. Ibid., p. 139.
84. Hull and Hoffer, *Roe v. Wade*, p. 168.
85. Weddington, *A Question of Choice*, pp. 138–141.
86. Weddington, *A Question of Choice*, p. 142.

Chapter 6

87. *Roe v. Wade*, 410 U.S. 113 (1973).
88. Hull and Hoffer, *Roe v. Wade*, p. 167..
89. Roe v. Wade 7.
90. Ibid.
91. Ibid.
92. Ibid.
93. Ibid.
94. Ibid.
95. Ibid.
96. Ibid.
97. Ibid.
98. Ibid.
99. Ibid.
100. Ibid.
101. Ibid.
102. Ibid.
103. Ibid.
104. Ibid.
105. Ibid.
106. Ibid.

Chapter 7

107. Weddington, *A Question of Choice*, p. 150.
108. McCorvey, *I Am Roe*, p. 150.
109. Weddington, *A Question of Choice*, p. 150.
110. Ibid., pp. 168–169.
111. Jane E. Brody, "Questions Left Unanswered by Ruling on Abortion," *New York Times*, January 24, 1973, p. 14.
112. Quoted in Brody, "Questions Left Unanswered," p. 14.
113. Hull and Hoffer, *Roe v. Wade*, p. 189.
114. "Buckley Pushes Curb on Abortion," *New York Times*, June 1, 1973, p. 12.
115. Quoted in Weddington, *A Question of Choice*, p. 171.
116. Carolyn Gerster, "A Brief History of the NRLC," *Life Lines* (January–February 2003): p. 3. http://www.azrtl.org.
117. Ibid.
118. "Abortion Foes to Seek Ban by Amending Constitution," *New York Times*, June 12, 1973, p. 21.
119. Robert Reinhold, "Boston Indicts Doctors in Fetus Cases," *New York Times*, April 13, 1974, p. 1.
120. Quoted in "Fact Sheet, The Hyde Amendment," NCHLA Fact Sheets, National Committee for a Human Life Amendment. http://nchla.org.
121. Ibid.

122. "Access Denied: Origins of the Hyde Amendment and Other Restrictions on Public Funding for Abortion," American Civil Liberties Union, December 1, 1994. http://www.aclu.org.

123. D. Granberg, J. Burlison, "The Abortion Issue in the 1980 Elections," *Family Planning Perspectives* (September–October, 1983): p. 231.

124. "Republican Party Platform of 1980," The American Presidency Project. http://www.presidency.ucsb.edu.

125. Ibid.

126. Ibid.

127. "Democratic Party Platform of 1980."

Chapter 8

128. "Testimony of Hon. Sandra Day O'Connor, Nominated to be Associate Justice of the U.S. Supreme Court," Supreme Court Nomination Hearings (1971–forward). GPO Access. http://www.gpoaccess.gov/congress/senate/judiciary.

129. Fred Barbash, "O'Connor Approved By Senate Committee," *Washington Post*, September 16, 1981, p. A2.

130 Hull and Hoffer, *Roe v. Wade*, pp. 215–216.

131. *Bellotti v. Baird*, 428 U.S. 132 (1976).

132. Sandra Day O'Connor, Dissenting Opinion, *Akron v. Akron Center for Reproductive Health*, 462 U.S. 416 (1983).

133. Hull and Hoffer, *Roe v. Wade*, p. 229.

134. Ibid., p. 231.

135. Ibid., p. 238.

136. Ibid.

137. Interview with Kathryn Kolbert, *Frontline*, PBS. http://www.pbs.org/wgbh.

138. Jill Nelson, "Abortion Foes Sense 'A New Wind Blowing,'" *Washington Post*, January 23, 1990, p. B1.

139. Joan Biskupic, "America's Longest War," *Washington Post* (January 22, 1993): p. A1.

140. William Booth, "Doctor Killed During Abortion Protest," *Washington Post*, March 11, 1993; "Michael Griffin Murders Dr. David Gunn," Christian Life Resources. http://www.christianlife resources.com.

141. Paul J. Hill, "Defending the Defenseless," on The Army of God web site. http://www.armyof-god.com/PHill_ShortShot.html.

142. Laurence Finer, quoted in "An Overview of Abortion in the United States," Guttmacher Institute Media Kit, http://www.guttmacher.org/media/presskits/2005/06/28/abor-tionoverview.html.

143. Partial Birth Abortion Ban Act of 2003. http://news.findlaw.com/hdocs/docs/abortion/2003s3.html.

144. "Stem Cell Information," National Institutes of Health. http://stemcells.nih.gov.

145. "Who Is Paul Hill?" The Army of God web site. http://www.armyofgod.com/Paulhillindex.html.

Glossary

abortion   The premature death of a fetus within the mother's uterus; often used to specify fetal expulsion intentionally caused by chemical, mechanical, or surgical means.

appeal   The right to request that a higher court reconsider a case judged in a lower court; appeals move from district court to circuit court, from circuit court to federal court, and from federal court to the U.S. Supreme Court, whose judgment is final.

brief   A formally structured document presented by an attorney expressing the argument of a case soon to be heard in court.

canon law   The laws expressed by the church, usually the Roman Catholic Church, having influence but not standing in civil courts in England and the United States.

class action   A lawsuit brought to court on behalf of a class of people, all of whom are argued to have suffered the same wrongdoing.

common law   The rules generally followed by the people throughout English history, which form the core of English and American law.

due process   The constitutional right of every U.S. citizen, protected by the Fourteenth Amendment, to a fair and equitable trial in a court of law.

embryo   Medically defined as the fertilized ovum through the eighth week of growth.

fetus   Medically defined as the unborn offspring after the eighth week of growth.

moot   For reasons of law, not worthy of consideration.

partial-birth abortion   A late-term medical procedure requiring the extraction of fetal brain contents before expulsion of fetus from uterus.

penumbra   In constitutional law, a set of rights not specifically named but implicitly included within a more generally named right; a halo of rights implied by a central, named right.

precedent   A past judicial decision on a related topic that may bear weight in a case under discussion.

quickening   An archaic term denoting the point in pregnancy when the mother feels movement of the fetus; in legal history, a landmark moment past which abortions are often outlawed.

trimester   Division of a time frame into thirds; in abortion law, the division of a pregnancy into three equal parts, each about three months long.

undue burden   A legal term indicating the point beyond which a citizen's constitutional rights are illegally limited by federal, state, or municipal law.

viability   The ability of a fetus to survive independently outside its mother's womb; in U.S. law, sometimes cited as the moment at which state responsibility for the rights of the fetus begins.

Bibliography

"Abortion Foes to Seek Ban by Amending Constitution." *New York Times*, June 12, 1973, p. 21.

"Abortion Law Protest in Paris." *New York Times*, April 5, 1971, p. 28.

"Abortion Requests Outrun Operations." *New York Times*, July 14, 1970, p. 13.

Akron v. Akron Center for Reproductive Health, 462 U.S. 416 (1983).

American Civil Liberties Union. "Access Denied: Origins of the Hyde Amendment and Other Restrictions on Public Funding for Abortion," December 1, 1994. http://www.aclu.org.

Barbash, Fred. "O'Connor Approved by Senate Committee." *Washington Post*, September 16, 1981, p. A2.

Bellotti v. Baird, 428 U.S. 132 (1976).

Biskupic, Joan. "America's Longest War." *Washington Post*, January 22, 1993, p. A1.

Booth, William. "Doctor Killed During Abortion Protest." *Washington Post*, March 11, 1993, p. A1.

Brody, Jane E. "Questions Left Unanswered by Ruling on Abortion." *New York Times*, January 24, 1973, p. 14.

"Buckley Pushes Curb on Abortion." *New York Times*, June 1, 1973, p. 12.

Commonwealth v. Daniel R. Wheeler, 315 Mass. 394 (1944).

Edmiston, Susan. "A Report on the Abortion Capital of the Country." *New York Times*, August 10, 1971, p. 19.

Gerster, Carolyn, Md. "A Brief History of NRLC." *Life Lines* 29, no. 1 (January–February 2003): pp. 3–4.

Granberg, D., and J. Burlison. "The Abortion Issue in the 1980 Elections." *Family Planning Perspectives* (September–October 1983).

Griswold v. Connecticut, 381 U.S. 479 (1965).

Hamilton, Edith, and Huntington Cairns, eds. *The Collected Dialogues of Plato*. Princeton, N.J.: Princeton University Press, 1961.

"Hippocratic Oath—Classical Version." Ludwig Edelstein, trans. *NOVA Online*. http://www.pbs.org/wgbh/nova/doctors/oath_classical.html.

Howe, Marvine. "Vatican Denounces Italian Senate Bill Legalizing Abortion." *New York Times*, August 10, 1971, p. 7.

Hull, N.E.H., and Peter Charles Hoffer, *Roe v. Wade: The Abortion Rights Controversy in American History*. Lawrence: University Press of Kansas, 2001.

Kolbert, Kathryn. "The Last Abortion Clinic" (interview). *Frontline*. http://www.pbs.org/wgbh.

Lord Ellenborough's Act, 43 Geo. 3, C. 58.

"Michael Griffin Murders Dr. David Gunn." Christian Life Resources, February 17, 1994. http://www.christianliferesources.com.

McCorvey, Norma, with Andy Meisler. *I Am Roe: My Life, Roe v. Wade, and Freedom of Choice*. New York: HarperCollins, 1994.

National Committee for a Human Life Amendment. "Fact Sheet: The Hyde Amendment." http://nchla.org.

National Institutes of Health. Stem Cell Information. http://stemcells.nih.gov.

Nelson, Jill. "Abortion Foes Sense 'A New Wind Blowing.'" *Washington Post*, January 23, 1990, p. B1.

The New Oxford Annotated Bible. New York: Oxford University Press, 1994.

"Nixon Abortion Statement." *New York Times*, April 4, 1971, p. 28.

Olmstead v. United States, 277 U.S. 438, 478 (1928).

Partial Birth Abortion Ban Act of 2003, 108th Congress, 1st Session.

The People v. Leon Phillip Belous, 71 Cal.2d 954, 80 Cal.Rptr. 354 (1969).

Poe v. Ullman, 367 U.S. 497 (1961).

Reinhold, Robert. "Boston Indicts Doctors in Fetus Cases." *New York Times*, April 13, 1974, p. 1.

Religious Institute on Sexual Morality, Justice, and Healing. "An Open Letter to Religious Leaders on Abortion as a Moral Decision." http://www.religiousinstitute.org.

Roe v. Wade, 410 U.S. 113 (1973).

Rubin, Eva R. *The Abortion Controversy: A Documentary History*. New York: Greenwood Press, 1994.

———. *Abortion, Politics, and the Courts: Roe v. Wade and Its Aftermath*. New York: Greenwood Press, 1987.

Scott, Mark S. "Quickening in the Common Law: The Legal Prec-
    edent *Roe* Attempted and Failed to Use" (note). *Michigan Law
    & Policy Review* (1996): p. 199.
Sibley, John. "69,000 Abortions in 6 Months Here." *New York Time*,
    February 7, 1971, p. 70.
"Testimony of Hon. Sandra Day O'Connor, Nominated to be
    Associate Justice of the U. S. Supreme Court," Supreme Court
    Nomination Hearings (1971–forward). GPO Access. http://www.
    gpoaccess.gov/congress/senate/judiciary.
"3 U.S. Judges Rule Laws on Abortion Invalid in Texas." *New York
    Times*, June 18, 1970, p. 37.
Weddington, Sarah. *A Question of Choice.* New York: Penguin
    Books, 1993.
"Who Is Paul Hill?" Army of God. http://www.armyofgod.com.
Woolley, John, and Gerhard Peters, eds. "Democratic Party
    Platform of 1980." The American Presidency Project.
    http://www.presidency.ucsb.edu.
———. "Republican Party Platform of 1980." The American
    Presidency Project. http://www.presidency.ucsb.edu.

Further Reading

Balkin, J.M., ed. *What Roe v. Wade Should Have Said: The Nation's Top Legal Experts Rewrite America's Most Controversial Decision.* New York: New York University Press, 2005.

Biskupic, Joan. *Sandra Day O'Connor: How the First Woman on the Supreme Court Became Its Most Influential Justice.* New York: Ecco (HarperCollins), 2005.

Gorney, Cynthia. *Articles of Faith: A Frontline History of the Abortion Wars.* New York: Simon & Schuster, 2000.

Greenhouse, Linda. *Becoming Justice Blackmun: Harry Blackmun's Supreme Court Journey.* New York: Times Books, 2006.

Ide, Arthur Frederick. *Abortion Handbook: The History, Legal Progress, Practice and Psychology of Abortion.* Las Colinas, Tex.: Liberal Press, 1988.

McCorvey, Norma, with Gary Wade. *Won by Love: Norma McCorvey, Jane Roe of Roe v. Wade, Shares Her New Conviction for Life.* Nashville, Tenn.: Thomas Nelson, 1998.

Nathanson, Bernard N., MD. *The Hand of God: A Journey from Death to Life by the Abortion Doctor Who Changed His Mind.* Washington, D.C.: Regnery, 2001.

Reagan, Leslie J. *When Abortion Was a Crime: Women, Medicine, and Law in the United States, 1867–1973.* Berkeley: University of California Press, 1998.

Riddle, John M. *Eve's Herbs: A History of Contraception and Abortion in the West.* Cambridge, Mass.: Harvard University Press, 1997.

Saletan, William. *Bearing Right: How Conservatives Won the Abortion War.* Berkeley: University of California Press, 2004.

Solinger, Rickie, ed. *Abortion Wars: A Half Century of Struggle, 1950–2000.* Berkeley: University of California Press, 1998.

Tribe, Laurence H. *The Clash of Absolutes.* New York: W.W. Norton, 1992.

Watkins, Christine, ed. *The Ethics of Abortion.* Detroit: Thomson Gale, 2005.

Picture Credits

Index

About the Author

Susan Tyler Hitchcock is the author of 12 nonfiction books and editor of many more. Her most recent publications are *Geography of Religion* (National Geographic, 2004) and *Mad Mary Lamb* (W. W. Norton, 2005). She is currently completing a cultural history of Frankenstein, to be published by W.W. Norton in 2007. She has written several other books for Chelsea House, including biographies of Sylvia Earle and Karen Horney. She has two adult children. She and her husband live near Charlottesville, Virginia, when they aren't sailing in the Caribbean.

About the Editor

Tim McNeese is an associate professor of history at York College in York, Nebraska. A prolific author of books for elementary, middle , and high school, and college readers, McNeese has published more than 80 books and educational materials over the past 20 years on subjects such as Alexander Hamilton to the siege of Masada. His writing has earned him a citation in the library reference work, *Something about the Author*. In 2005, his textbook *Political Revolutions of the 18th, 19th, and 20th Centuries* was published. Professor McNeese served as a consulting historian for the History Channel program, "Risk Takers, History Makers."